# A

# Rhetoric

# Handbook

for

English

1301

and

1302

First
Edition

Amarillo

College

English

Department

HAYDEN
HM
McNEIL

## Hayden-McNeil Sustainability

Hayden-McNeil's standard paper stock uses a minimum of 30% post-consumer waste. We offer higher % options by request, including a 100% recycled stock. Additionally, Hayden-McNeil Custom Digital provides authors with the opportunity to convert print products to a digital format. Hayden-McNeil is part of a larger sustainability initiative through Macmillan Higher Ed. Visit http://sustainability.macmillan.com to learn more.

Printed in the United States of America

10 9 8 7 6 5 4 3 2 1

ISBN 978-0-7380-5915-0

Hayden-McNeil Publishing
14903 Pilot Drive
Plymouth, MI 48170
www.hmpublishing.com

Sobey 5915-0 F13

# Table
# of
# Contents

# Contact Information

---

**DR. DAN FERGUSON, DEPARTMENT CHAIR**

Amarillo College
English Department
Ordway Hall Room 103D
PO Box 447
Amarillo, TX 79178-0001
(806) 371-5472
(806) 371-5399—fax
dwferguson@actx.edu

---

**DEPARTMENT OFFICE LOCATION**

Ordway Hall Room 103

---

**DEPARTMENT OFFICE PHONE**

(806) 371-5170

---

**WRITING LAB INFORMATION**

DEBBIE ORTEGA, ADMINISTRATIVE ASSISTANT
Amarillo College
English Department
Ordway Hall Room 103
PO Box 447
Amarillo, TX 79178-0001
(806) 371-5170
(806) 371-5399—fax
drortega@actx.edu

---

**WRITING LAB LOCATIONS**

Ordway Hall Room 101 & Ordway Hall Room 104
(806) 371-5174

---

**WRITERS' CORNER**

Ordway Hall Room 102
(806) 345-5580

---

**ENGLISH DEPARTMENT WEBSITE: http://www.actx.edu/english**

# Introduction

You have something to say. With this handbook, we in the Amarillo College English Department hope to help you say it better—in writing. We want you to develop a clear sense of purpose, a clear sense of audience, and a clear idea of the most effective means of getting your message across to your readers. The information contained in this handbook will help you become more confident in your writing and develop the skills that you need to say precisely what you want to say and to move your readers in the direction you want them to go. In short, we want you to develop the art of rhetoric. This handbook will help. Also, for access to additional helpful resources for 1301 and 1302, please visit the following site on the English Department homepage:

http://www.actx.edu/english/index.php?module=article&id=12=12

The Amarillo College English Department would like to thank the following people for creating and developing this handbook in 2005: Dr. Judith L. Carter, Dr. Dan Ferguson, Dwight Huber, Angie Siens Peoples, Dr. William Netherton, and Margie Waguespack.

# Resources for English 1301 and 1302

## ENGLISH DEPARTMENT PLAGIARISM POLICY (Revised 2013)

The English Department takes plagiarism seriously.

Plagiarism is defined as the following: the use of someone else's exact words that are neither quoted nor cited; paraphrasing someone else's words without citing them; or using someone else's research without citing it.

Student plagiarism in the Amarillo College English Department is internally tracked. To clarify, records will be kept in the Department of those students who have plagiarized. At the beginning of each new semester, the names of students who plagiarized the previous semester will be sent to all English Department faculty.

Plagiarism may receive a penalty of a zero. A subsequent infraction will be deemed a reason for expulsion from the class. At this point, the case will be referred to the Vice President of Student Affairs.

Note: Self-plagiarism will be discussed with the class by each instructor, and infractions for such are left up to the individual instructor's discretion.

## STEPS IN AVOIDING PLAGIARISM

1. Before trying to avoid plagiarism, it's important that you know its definition and what it looks like. Be sure to consult the pages in this course pack that deal with the definition of plagiarism and the policies governing it at Amarillo College.

2. If you do not understand exactly how to deal with information from a source, ask your instructor. He or she will be glad to talk to you about what plagiarism is and is not before you turn in the final draft. We all recognize that using sources correctly isn't the easiest thing in the world, especially with countless style recommendations by MLA, APA, and others. If you feel that you may be using a source incorrectly, bring the situation to your instructor's attention *before* the final draft of the paper is due.

3. Completing annotated bibliographies for your sources is a good way to avoid plagiarism. Also, it will help you to understand the source you are thinking about using and whether or not it will work in your essay. You will find directions on writing an annotated bibliography along with a sample in this course pack.

4. If you are using sources on the Internet, make sure that if you copy and paste material into your paper, you immediately put quotation marks around the exact words you are bringing into your paper, and go ahead and cite the

source parenthetically. Don't wait until later in the writing process. Often, students forget which words were theirs and which words belonged to the source, leading directly to plagiarism. Also, don't wait to create your works-cited page. As you bring in sources, add them to your works-cited page alphabetically. Doing so will keep you from scrambling at the last hour to find the source again.

5. When you paraphrase something from a source, be sure that you change the wording in the sentence and the way it is written. For example, in paraphrasing the previous sentence, you wouldn't start out with, "When you paraphrase... ." You would say, "Make sure to use different words and sentence structure when paraphrasing." Don't forget to tag the source, cite the source parenthetically, and list it on the works-cited page.

6. Do not quote a whole paragraph from another source in your paper. If you find a paragraph from a source that you are tempted to use in your paper, summarize it, introduce it with a tag, put it in your own words in the paper, cite the source parenthetically, and list it on the works-cited page. Long quotations are not normally recommended for a short paper, and it is extremely rare to quote a whole paragraph from another source.

7. When in doubt, cite the source. If you are using some ideas from the source, but you aren't using its exact words, you still need to introduce the ideas with a tag, cite the source parenthetically, and list it on the works-cited page.

8. Make absolutely clear who is saying the quote. Don't just insert a quotation into your paper. Be sure to use an attributive tag that lets the reader know who is saying the quotation. Often, you can use the title of the person or information about the person to provide credibility for the source, thus building your own credibility. For example, if you are writing a paper on a legal issue such as the rights of prisoners, and in your research you find a quotation from a Harvard Law professor who specializes in prison law, you would want to include her name and credentials when you quote her.

# WORDS AND PHRASES TO AVOID IN COLLEGE-LEVEL ACADEMIC WRITING

| | | |
|---|---|---|
| **Intensifiers** | These words are intended to emphasize an idea, but instead, they usually weaken it by using more words than necessary. Forceful writing uses as few words as possible to communicate the idea. | 1. very<br>2. actually<br>3. extremely<br>4. basically<br>5. really<br>6. quite<br>7. definitely<br>8. perfectly<br>9. a lot |
| **Superfluities** | These groups of words are unnecessary because unless readers are told otherwise, they safely assume that you are writing your own thoughts. | 1. I feel…<br>2. I believe…<br>3. I think…<br>4. In my opinion…<br>5. It seems to me…<br>6. I personally… |
| **Extravagancies** | These words should be saved for special occasions, and even then, they should be supported with specifics. | 1. great<br>2. super<br>3. wonderful<br>4. fantastic<br>5. terrific<br>6. !*<br>*(Exclamation points are rare in academic writing.) |
| **Absolutes** | These words often turn a generalization into a lie by indicating that a situation has no exceptions. | 1. always<br>2. never<br>3. none<br>4. invariably<br>5. everybody<br>6. anybody |
| **Vague Word Choices** | These words suggest that the writer did not care enough to think of an exact word. | 1. a lot (even worse—alot, which is never acceptable in formal writing)<br>2. find myself (himself, herself, etc.)<br>3. clichés ("You can't judge a book by its cover," "when push comes to shove," "as quiet as a mouse," or any other words that seem to be inseparable.)<br>4. sentences beginning with "there" or "it"<br>5. when it comes to<br>6. "there" in any situation in which it does not indicate a specific place (constructions like "Job-seekers can find a plenty of career choices out there," "Of course, there are many differences between,…" and "A child needs a parent to be there in times of trouble.")<br>7. needless to say<br>8. it goes without saying |

## MLA MANUSCRIPT PREPARATION

1. Use regular white paper, which is 8 ½ by 11 inches. Use lined paper for handwritten papers.

2. Never submit a handwritten paper from a spiral notebook if the page has tattered edges. If you must use spiral notebook paper, be sure to remove each tatter so that the left edge of the paper is totally smooth.

3. Write or print only on the front side of each paper.

4. Use black or dark blue ink for handwritten papers. Print out your typed essays with black ink.

5. Leave a one-inch margin on all four sides of the paper.

6. Double-space everything, no more and no less.

7. If you are using a computer to write the paper, use a size 12 font that looks like something you might see in a published book or magazine. Arial, Courier, and Times New Roman work well. The entire paper, including the heading and the title, should use the same font.

8. Justify only the left side.

9. In the upper right corner of each page, one-half inch from the top of the paper, place your last name and the page number.

10. Use the conventional MLA heading on the first page only. On the upper left corner of the paper, one inch from the top of the paper, write your name. Skip a line; all work in the MLA style is double-spaced, including the heading. On the next line, write the instructor's name. On the following line, allowing for double-spacing, write the course number followed by a hyphen and the section number. For example, if you are in Comp 1, your course number is English 1301. If you are in section 052, then the third line of the heading should look like this: English 1301-052. Finally, on the last line of the heading, place the date in day-month-year style: 20 August 2012.

11. Use only one double space between the heading and the title. The title should be centered on the next line. If the title is original, do not place it in quotation marks, and do not underline it.

12. Use both uppercase and lowercase letters.

## Sample Page 1 of MLA-Style Paper

Jane Smith

Professor Jones

English 1301-052

1 September 2012

The Real Robin Hood

Through the years, Hollywood has produced several movies about the hero of Sherwood Forest, Robin Hood. Douglas Fairbanks, Sr. had great success with his silent version, *Robin Hood*, in 1922; and, of course, Kevin Costner made his politically correct, revisionist version, *Robin Hood: Prince of Thieves*, in 1991. Still, the best movie ever produced about the Robin Hood legends was the 1938 masterpiece *The Adventures of Robin Hood*, starring the king of swashbucklers, Errol Flynn.

One reason *The Adventures of Robin Hood* succeeds is the superb cast. Besides Flynn, the movie features Claude Rains, one of the most versatile actors of the silver screen, as the dastardly Prince John. Cruel and calculating, Rains's Prince John is topped as a villain only by Basil Rathbone as Sir Guy of Gisbourne. Rathbone (best known these days as a good guy for the roles he played as Sherlock Holmes) is remarkably effective playing a character who is at once childish in his over-sensitivity and ruthless in his revenge. Olivia de Havilland is the most beautiful—and the most independent—Marian to come out of Hollywood.

## PROOFREADING CHECKLIST FOR FINAL COPIES

Before you turn in the final copy of your essay (which will be graded for content, organization, and grammar), proofread your essay carefully, using this checklist as a guide.

### CONTENT

- Does your essay contain a fully developed introduction with a clear thesis statement?

- Do you have at least two fully developed body paragraphs with clear topic sentences?

- Do you have a fully developed conclusion?

- Is each paragraph unified? (Does it stay on topic, supporting the topic sentence?)

- Is each paragraph coherent? (Does it flow logically from sentence to sentence?)

- Is each paragraph fully developed? (Is the topic sentence adequately supported?)

- Are there clear transitions from paragraph to paragraph?

- Does each portion of the essay support the thesis statement?

- Does the essay contain specific details and vivid examples rather than vague, general language?

- Does the essay meet the required length?

### ORGANIZATION

- Is the thesis statement the last sentence in the introduction? (For a narrative essay, the thesis may appear in the conclusion.)

- If the thesis statement contains the points to be covered, are these points presented in the same order in your essay?

- Are your points presented in a logical, effective order? (Remember that your most important point should be saved for the last body paragraph. Also, some points need to be read first before other points make sense.)

- If this is a comparison/contrast essay, does your essay follow one of the recommended organizational patterns—either subject-by-subject or point-by-point? If this is a descriptive essay and you provide a physical description of a person, does this come before you discuss personality traits? If this is an argument essay, have you included an awareness of opponents' views in a logical location? Is your argument organized around reasons for your stand, with evidence organized under each reason? If this is a narrative essay, does your re-creation of events follow a logical, chronological order without any confusing gaps?

## GRAMMAR/SPELLING

- Have you used SpellCheck? Have you proofread for spelling errors AFTER SpellCheck (which cannot distinguish between words such as *form* and *from*, for example)?

- Proofread for sentence fragments (incomplete thoughts that either need to be attached to a nearby sentence or made complete by adding missing material).

*Fragments:*
Because it was raining. Judy decided to stay home.
Not only Judy but Tom too.

*Corrections:*
Because it was raining, Judy decided to stay home.
Tom decided to stay home, too.

- Proofread for run-on sentences and comma splices. (Run-ons are two complete sentences joined with no punctuation. Comma splices are two complete sentences joined by only a comma.)

*Run-on:*
On Saturday, Tara went to the mall then she ate at Sonic.

*Comma splice:*
On Saturday, Tara went to the mall, then she ate at Sonic.

*Corrections:*
On Saturday, Tara went to the mall, **and** then she ate at Sonic.

On Saturday, Tara went to the mall. Then she ate at Sonic.

On Saturday, Tara went to the mall; then she ate at Sonic.

- Proofread for subject-verb agreement errors. (Singular subjects require singular verbs; plural subjects require plural verbs.)

*Subject-verb agreement errors:*

The **crowd** of noisy demonstrators **were** attracting attention.

**Inflation**, as well as taxes, **influence** voters.

There **is** many possible **candidates**.

Either Gail or her sister **know** what happened.

*Corrections:*

The **crowd** of noisy demonstrators **was** attracting attention.

**Inflation**, as well as taxes, **influences** voters.

There **are** many possible **candidates**.

Either Gail or her sister **knows** what happened. (Either Gail knows OR her sister knows.)

- Proofread for pronoun-antecedent agreement errors. (A pronoun referring to a singular word must be singular; a pronoun referring to a plural word must be plural.)

*Pronoun-antecedent agreement errors:*

Each **student** should bring **their** textbook.

Either Tim or John will be giving **their** speech.

*Corrections:*

Each **student** should bring **his or her** textbook.

**Students** should bring **their textbooks**.

Either Tim or John will be giving **his** speech. (Either Tim will give his speech OR John will give his speech.)

- Other common grammatical errors to check for: pronoun case errors, dangling/misplaced modifiers, inconsistent verb tense, improper verb forms or improper pluralization, comma errors, and capitalization errors.

# WRITE A RESPONSE PAPER USING THE MLA FORMAT

Most instructors in the English Department at AC will ask for a response paper, typically over a reading assignment. Your response paper should include **a summary, a response, and a work-cited page**. Depending on the length and the complexity of the text, a summary and a response should have at least 450 words. Both the summary and response should be written in third person unless an option is indicated by the instructor.

The purpose of a **summary** is to provide a reader with a short version of the main ideas. Most of the details are omitted so that important information, which reflects the author's original text, is provided. In a summary, include the following information:

- Include the author's name and the title of the text.

- Include the main point(s) of the text.

- Include two direct quotations or paraphrases with parenthetical citations in the summary section. Use transitions to introduce concrete details.

A **response** is the reader's reaction to the author's original text. A response may have factual information cited from the original text. There are four types of responses. A writer may select one type, or he/she may include steps from each type of responses.

- How effective is the text? The response should analyze key factors such as the main idea, organization, style, tone, and voice.

- Does the audience agree or disagree with the author's presentation? What is the audience's reaction to the text? Evidence from the text must be provided.

- What is the interpretation of the text? Explain key points.

- Reflect on the text. The writer responds to the text by reflecting on his/her observations and experiences and how they relate to the text.

Do not forget to include a separate work-cited page.

## HERE IS A PASSAGE FROM HENRY DAVID THOREAU'S ORIGINAL ESSAY ON WALDEN, 1854:

*"Where I Lived, and What I Lived For"*

I went to the woods because I wished to live deliberately, to front only the essential facts of life, and see if I could not learn what it had to teach, and not, when I came to die, discover that I had not lived. I did not wish to live what was not life, living is so dear; nor did I wish to practise resignation, unless it was quite necessary. I wanted to live deep and suck out all the marrow of life, to live so sturdily and Spartan-like as to put to rout all that was not life, to cut a broad swath and shave close, to drive life into a corner, and reduce it to its lowest terms, and, if it proved to be mean, why then to get the whole and genuine meanness of it, and publish its meanness to the world; or if it were sublime, to know it by experience, and be able to give a true account of it in my next excursion. For most men, it appears to me, are in a strange uncertainty about it, whether it is of the devil or of God, and have *somewhat hastily* concluded that it is the chief end of man here to "glorify God and enjoy him forever."

### *Summary*

In the essay, "Where I Lived, and What I Lived for," Henry David Thoreau goes into the woods to experience life in the simplest form by learning what nature can teach him so that when he dies, he would not regret that he did not live. Thoreau says, "I did not wish to live what was not life, living is so dear; nor did I wish to practice resignation, unless it was quite necessary" (343). Thoreau's life in the woods would not consist of the details of a complicated lifestyle; he would be a soldier who lives on limited essentials. Whether the experience is good or bad, Thoreau wants to share that experience in his next writing. The author says that a person's existence is to praise God and to serve God forever (Thoreau 344). Thoreau lives in the woods to find out the meaning of life because he does not want to be caught up in what others have made life to be.

### *Response*

Henry David Thoreau's essay emphasizes the importance of living a simple life. He must have experienced a stressful life of living with what others called "essentials." A materialistic society always finds itself hurrying to places, always working to fulfill nonessential needs, and always trying to keep up with the latest fashions or styles. Life needs to be simple; no one needs to be in a hurry by trying to fill every second of time with activities. If a person is here to "glorify God..." (344), then a person also needs to enjoy, according to Thoreau, what God has provided him or her. To appreciate the good things in life, a person needs to unclutter his or her lifestyle and be closer to nature.

### *Work Cited*

Thoreau, Henry David. "Where I Lived and What I Lived For." *The Portable Thoreau*. Ed. Carl Bode. NY: Penguin, 1947. 334-335. Print.

## HOW TO FIND AND DOCUMENT SOURCES USING MLA STYLE

### FINDING RELIABLE SOURCES ON THE INTERNET

One reliable source for full-text newspaper, magazine, and journal articles is *Bnet* at *www.findarticles.com*. Be sure to narrow your search key words as much as possible, or you may end up with too many items in your search results.

Next, you might want to go the Lynn Library's homepage and look at the "Find an Article" section. Here, you'll find several databases, some of which contain full-text articles you can print. One helpful database for argument essays is *Opposing Viewpoints*. Other helpful databases include *CQ Researcher* and *TOPICsearch*. Use key words related to your argument topic to search these databases, such as "Arguments Against Death Penalty."

You can also do a general keyword search on the Internet. You might use "arguments for _____" and then fill in the topic you are covering, such as capital punishment, drug testing student athletes, etc. Type this phrase in the search box of any search engine. Look over your search results carefully to determine who has generated the information. If a website does not have a clear, authoritative author or organization behind it, then you cannot necessarily trust the information you find there.

*Make sure you find out and keep any authors' names, website editors' names, website titles, database titles, article titles, dates, web addresses, etc.* You will have to document this information when you use outside information in your essay.

## HOW TO DOCUMENT OUTSIDE SOURCES IN YOUR ARGUMENT ESSAY USING MLA STYLE

If you use statistics, facts, comments or any other information that you find in an outside source, you must give credit to the author/originator of that information. Otherwise, you commit **plagiarism**, a serious academic offense. The only exception to this rule is common knowledge—information that cannot be attributed to one person or source and which is commonly known. For example, the fact that the earth is round or that the Boston Red Sox won the World Series would be considered common knowledge.

*If you use outside sources in your paper, you need to take three important steps:*

1. **Introduce** all borrowed information, whether a direct quotation in quotation marks or a summary of statistics and research. (Underlining has been added to indicate the introduction.)

   According to Dr. James Smith, Professor of Psychology at Brown University, "Many bright students perform poorly on standardized tests" (123).

   As a UCLA study demonstrated, 20% of students have some form of test anxiety (Jones 10).

   One researcher has found a dramatic rise in trips to the nurse's office during standardized testing (Townsend 25).

2. Provide at least the source's <u>**last name**</u> and the <u>**page number**</u> (for a print source) when using an outside source. In English and other humanities classes, use the MLA (Modern Language Association) method of documenting sources. (Bolding has been added to the documentation for emphasis.)

One psychology professor concluded, "Many bright students perform poorly on standardized tests" (**Smith 12**).

Psychology Professor Dr. James Smith concluded, "Many bright students perform poorly on standardized tests" (**12**).

For an electronic source with no page numbers provided:

According to one psychology professor, "Many bright students perform poorly on standardized tests" (**Smith**).

3. Create a **works-cited page** as the last page of your essay. For **each** source cited in your paper, you must have a corresponding works-cited entry. Works-cited entries are arranged alphabetically by what comes first in the entry.

Smith, James. *Standardized Testing Is Overrated.* New York: Prentice, 2004. Print.

Townsend, Sarah. "Research on Standardized Testing." *Education Journal* 15.2 (1999): 33–45. *Opposing Viewpoints.* Web. 25 Sept. 2003.

---

## INCORPORATING QUOTATIONS

### I. GENERAL INFORMATION

A poor research paper or critique of a literary work is often a scissors-and-paste collection of lengthy quotations looming up at intervals in student prose. Stringing together a mass of quotations <u>without giving the relevance</u> for their inclusion is unacceptable.

In a superior paper, more material states <u>the student writer's opinion</u> with paraphrased evidence for support than material directly quoted from the original source.

The quotations that are used are gracefully <u>blended</u> with the text instead of standing alone with no connection to what precedes or to what follows. No quotation should stand alone in its own sentence without properly <u>introducing</u> it with either the point you are making or with an example of the point.

## II. PUNCTUATION NEEDED WHEN INTRODUCING QUOTATIONS

### A. Introducing Quotations with a Colon

A colon is a common but rather formal way of introducing a quotation when the quotation is preceded by a complete sentence rather than the word *says* or *writes* or *tells*. The following are acceptable uses of the colon with quotations:

> Milton rejects overinnocence as follows: "I cannot praise a fugitive and cloistered virtue, unexercised and unbreathed, that never sallies out" (25).

> Milton rejects overinnocence: "I cannot praise a fugitive and cloistered virtue, unexercised and unbreathed, that never sallies out" (25).

### B. Introducing Quotations with a Comma

A quotation is preceded by a comma when the quotation is preceded by such words as says, states, writes, or tells.

> John Milton writes, "I cannot praise a fugitive and cloistered virtue, unexercised and unbreathed, that never sallies out" (25).

### C. Introducing Quotations without Preceding Them with Punctuation

When a quotation is an integral part of your own sentence (often a subject, direct object, or a modifying phrase), a comma is not needed.

> Milton describes naive innocence as "a fugitive and cloistered virtue, unexercised and unbreathed, that never sallies out" (25).

> The display of wealth, according to Veblen, is "a means of reputability" (117).

When the word *that* immediately precedes a quotation, a comma is seldom necessary.

> Milton writes that "he cannot praise a fugitive and cloistered virtue, unexercised and unbreathed, that never sallies forth" (25).

## III. ACCEPTABLE WORDS TO USE IN INTRODUCING QUOTATIONS

If you introduce a quotation with a verb, do not overwork *says* and *writes*, but look for synonyms. For example:

| | | |
|---|---|---|
| acknowledges | discusses | notes |
| affirms | emphasizes | observes |
| agrees | explains | relates |
| argues | expresses | remarks |
| asserts | implies | reports |
| believes | insists | states |
| cautions | maintains | suggests |
| comments | mentions | thinks |
| declares | | |

# MLA PARENTHETICAL CITATIONS

1. **AUTHOR NOT NAMED IN THE SENTENCE**

    When you have not already named the author in the sentence, provide the author's last name and the page number(s), with no punctuation between them, in parentheses.

    One critic concludes that "women impose a distinctive construction on moral problems, seeing moral dilemmas in terms of conflicting responsibilities" (Gilligan 105).

2. **AUTHOR NAMED IN THE SENTENCE**

    Critic Carol Gilligan concludes that "women impose a distinctive construction on moral problems, seeing moral dilemmas in terms of conflicting responsibilities" (105).

3. **A WORK WITH TWO OR THREE AUTHORS**

    Frieden and Sagalyn write, "The poor and the minorities were the leading victims of highway and renewal programs" (29).

    Or

    One source suggests, "The poor and the minorities were the leading victims of highway and renewal programs" (Frieden and Sagalyn 29).

4. **A WORK WITH MORE THAN THREE AUTHORS**

    It took the combined forces of the Americans, Europeans, and Japanese to break the rebel siege of Peking in 1900 (Lopez et al. 362).

5. **A WORK BY AN AUTHOR OF TWO OR MORE WORKS**

    If your works-cited list has two or more articles by the same author, give a shortened version of the title after the author's name. This article is entitled "The Arts and Human Development."

    "Children use appropriate gestures to reinforce their stories" (Gardener, "Arts" 144–45).

6. **AN INDIRECT SOURCE**

    This is a quotation used by the author of your source.

    George Davino maintains that "even small children have vivid ideas about nuclear energy" (qtd. in Boyd 22).

7. **CITATIONS WITH ELLIPSIS (A SPACE SHOULD BE PLACED BETWEEN EACH PERIOD)**

    One observer says, "American manufacturers must bear some blame for the current recession..." (Rosenbaum 12).

8.  A QUOTATION WITHIN A QUOTATION

> For quotes inside quotes, use a single quotation mark.
>
> Richardson writes, "The macabre is beautifully unexpected in William's Faulkner's 'A Rose for Emily'" (205).

9.  QUOTES WHERE THE ACKNOWLEDGMENT PHRASE COMES AT THE END OF THE SENTENCE

> "To lengthen thy life, lessen thy meals," wrote Ben Franklin (qtd. in Johnson 233).

10. ACKNOWLEDGMENT PHRASE INTERRUPTING THE QUOTATION

> "It is healthier," writes one biologist, "to be ten pounds overweight" (Adams 23).

11. LONG QUOTATIONS (4 LINES OR MORE)

> Jane Aaron suggests:
>
> Every time you borrow the words, facts, or ideas of others, you must document the source—that is, supply a reference (or documentation) telling readers that you borrowed the material and where you borrowed it from. Editors and teachers in most academic disciplines require special documentation formats (or styles) in their scholarly journals. (210)

12. QUOTATIONS THAT NEED TO BE CLARIFIED

> Use brackets [ ] when adding words or when changing words to clarify a direct quotation.
>
> *Pronoun Example:*
>
> With Heaven above and Faith below, I will yet stand firm against the devil. (Original quote)
>
> Goodman Brown claims that "with Heaven above and Faith below, [he] will yet stand firm against the devil" (Hawthorne 760).
>
> *Punctuation & Capitalization Example:*
>
> He was a gentleman from sole to crown,
>
> Clean favored, and imperially slim. (Original lines of poetry)
>
> Richard Cory, "[c]lean favored, and imperially slim" (Robinson 86), is from head to toe a gentleman.

13. AN ELECTRONIC SOURCE WITH NO PAGE NUMBERS ASSIGNED

> In the Web article, "Elizabeth Barrett Browning," one critic asserts that "Browning blends irony and pathos to prick the conscience of her reader" (Stevens).

## 14. AN ELECTRONIC SOURCE WITH NO AUTHOR'S NAME PROVIDED

If an electronic source is reputable but no specific author is provided, use a shortened form of the source title in the parentheses following the borrowed information. If the source is an article, put the title in quotation marks. If the source is a book, italicize the title.

A 2002 study at Yale University found that most high school teachers would prefer to eliminate high stakes standardized testing ("Standardized Testing").

---

# HOW TO PARAPHRASE

A paraphrase is one way to borrow from a source. When you paraphrase, you take someone else's idea and change how it was worded by putting it into YOUR WORDS. A good paraphrase, as you will see, expresses the borrowed idea in a completely different way. But being able to produce such a paraphrase is hard. Why? Those who are learning this skill for the first time often believe that any kind of change is sufficient. Your paraphrase, however, has to be original in its expression, though obviously the idea being expressed belongs to another. So here are three things to keep in mind as you paraphrase:

- Change more than just the order of words, phrases, and clauses in the passage you are paraphrasing. Some writers will rearrange sentences and leave the paraphrase at that. A paraphrase like that will be too close to the original, often using similar wording.

- Paraphrasing involves much more than merely finding synonyms. First, a synonym may have a connotation that does not fit. For example, a cook who is stirring soup probably should not end up stimulating the soup, though to *stir* and to *stimulate* are synonymous. Second, if all you are doing is replacing each word in the original passage with a synonym, the final paraphrase will be too close to the original.

- You may use exact language from the original, especially if there's a word or phrase that is distinct and cannot be accurately changed. But if you use exact language from the original, whether it's more than three words in consecutive order OR distinct phrasing, make sure you quote it.

Why would you use a paraphrase, especially if it is such a hard skill to get right? After all, we have other techniques for borrowing from sources, such as summarizing and quoting. Paraphrasing, however, allows us

- to establish *ethos* by demonstrating our mastery of the material.

- to avoid quoting bland, highly technical, or audience-inappropriate passages from sources.

- to vary the style of source integration.

When you paraphrase, however, you should adhere to the guidelines below:

- Do not alter the original meaning of the passage you are paraphrasing.

- Do not muddy your paraphrase with your bias, particularly when you are using a paraphrase to outline an opponent's position.

- Make sure your paraphrase stands alone. If your reader deems it necessary to go to the original passage for clarification, then your paraphrase is ineffective.

- Make sure your paraphrase covers all of the meaning conveyed by the original passage.

So now let's work on paraphrase. Here is a passage from Tim Wu's "An Ode to Weightlifting, My New Favorite Olympic Sport" *(http://www.slate.com/ id/2197254/entry/2197698/)*:

> The simplicity of the lift also differentiates the sport from boxing and judo, which have moments of absolute glory but also have lots of mess in between. Real boxing isn't like *Rocky*, where every punch is perfect and lands with a satisfying thud. Even a beautiful sport like soccer has its share of ugliness (sometimes 89 minutes' worth). But real weightlifting is perfect. Either there's a gigantic amount of weight over your head or there isn't.

Here's a bad paraphrase that not only stays too close to the original but fails to quote exact language:

> ~~The lift's simplicity~~ makes the sport ~~different than boxing or judo~~, which both are ~~absolutely glorious~~ at times but mostly messy. ~~Unlike *Rocky*, true boxing is not perfect and every punch does not land~~ with a <u>wonderful</u> thud. ~~Though beautiful, even soccer can be ugly~~—sometimes for most of a game. *Weightlifting*, on the other hand, *is perfect*. The weightlifter ~~either lifts the weight over his head or he does not~~.

~~Too close~~

*Exact language*

<u>Inaccurate</u>

Plus, the writer did not mention the author or article. So this paraphrase is also guilty of undocumented plagiarism. A better paraphrase would be:

> Tim Wu, in "An Ode to Weightlifting, My New Favorite Olympic Sport," obviously appreciates the "moments of absolute glory" he finds in boxing and judo, but in his mind these two sports, when compared to weightlifting, are not nearly as enjoyable due to "lots of mess in between." Soccer, known around the world as the beautiful game, also fails to live up to Wu's expectations. Moreover, he takes issue with the false film portrayals of sports like boxing, which in reality, he argues, is dissimilar

to boxing movies like *Rocky*. In the final analysis, according to Wu, weightlifting's perfection is derived from "the simplicity of the lift" and the end result: "Either there's a gigantic amount of weight over your head or there isn't."

Certainly, this paraphrase is much longer than the original passage. That is okay. Also notice that the writer incorporates spot quotations throughout—even a formal colon quotation at the end. That, too, is okay. You definitely do not want to force a paraphrase by avoiding quotations altogether. But notice the overall effect of the paraphrase: Is there any doubt that the writer owns this material?

So do practice your paraphrasing skills. Make sure you adhere to the rules. Always cite the author and/or article. And if you have any questions, let your instructor review your paraphrase ahead of time.

## HOW PURPOSE DETERMINES THE STRUCTURE OF AN ESSAY

Students often ask how many paragraphs their essays should have. Most essays written in Freshman Composition I contain 4–6 paragraphs. All essays written for Freshman Composition I and Freshman Composition II must include an introduction, a thesis statement, body paragraphs, and a conclusion. However, the most significant factor determining the particular structure of an essay is the essay's PURPOSE.

If your purpose is to PERSUADE someone to accept your point of view, you are going to structure your essay quite differently than you would if your purpose is to COMPARE AND CONTRAST two subjects or to NARRATE an incident that had an impact on you.

For example, let's say that you are assigned the general topic "Smoking" and must decide on a purpose and audience for your essay. The purpose and the audience together is called the RHETORICAL SITUATION. In other words, WHY are you writing this essay and FOR WHOM are you writing it? If you decide that your purpose is to persuade Amarillo voters to vote for the public smoking ban, then it would make sense to give background information on this controversial issue in the introduction and then present your stand as your thesis. Your body paragraphs could be organized around the reasons for your stand, with a variety of evidence to support each reason. You would choose evidence and appeals that you think would be effective with your audience, Amarillo voters who disagree with you or who are unsure of their position. Then your conclusion should strongly reinforce your stand to end your essay on a convincing note.

If you decide that your purpose is to compare/contrast two techniques for quitting smoking to examine their effectiveness for different types of smokers, and your audience is smokers interested in quitting, you would structure your essay differently. For example, you might organize your body paragraphs in a subject-by-subject fashion, first examining one method and then turning to the second method in the next body paragraph. In your conclusion, you could conclude that one method seems more suited for a certain type of smoker while the other method might suit another type.

On the other hand, you might decide that your purpose is to narrate or tell about an incident in your life when you gave in to peer pressure, smoked cigarettes, and learned something about your desire for approval. Your audience could be your classmates. In this case, you would probably want to provide a biographical context in your introduction, letting the audience know how old you were and what you were like when this incident took place. Instead of putting a thesis in your introduction, you might not want to "give away" the point of the story until you tell it. Therefore, you could structure this narrative in chronological order, re-creating the incident, step-by-step, for the audience. You could divide your paragraphs based on shifts in time rather than separate points, reasons, or subjects, as in other types of essays. In the conclusion, you could "wrap up" the aftermath of the incident and reveal how it impacted you. Your point for telling the story could be summed up in a thesis in the conclusion.

In Freshman Composition II, you will probably have to write an essay or longer paper analyzing a work of literature. Sometimes students have trouble figuring out how to structure this kind of literary analysis since it is usually different from the writing they did in Freshman Composition I. However, think of literary analysis as a type of argument. If you are asked to assert an opinion about a work of literature, whether about the theme, a character, or a conflict, you must defend this opinion, just as you do in an argument essay. This opinion would appear in your thesis statement as a direct assertion.

If your purpose is to show how Emily Grierson in "A Rose for Emily" represents the Old South, then you could structure your essay around evidence in the short story that supports this opinion. For example, your first body paragraph might focus on the description of Emily as submerged in a stagnant body of water to show how she, like the Old South, is resistant to change. In your second body paragraph, you might focus on her black manservant, Tobe, to show how her reliance on him mirrors the Old South's reliance on slavery. If your purpose is to show that a theme in "Young Goodman Brown" seems to be the inability to accept an imperfect faith, then you might focus on the pink ribbon in one body paragraph, Brown's reaction to the traveler's statements about his family in another body paragraph, and Brown's rejection of his wife Faith in another.

You are not limited to three or four body paragraphs since your purpose is to show that you have strong evidence for your opinion about a work. You should continue to present evidence in well-developed paragraphs until you feel that you have convincingly supported your thesis. If your audience is your instructor, then you should assume that he or she is familiar with the work and should not spend time on plot summary. If you keep your purpose in mind, you will stay focused on supporting your opinion about the literary work and will bring in only effective evidence from the work itself and from outside sources, if required.

## THE RHETORICAL PRECIS

A rhetorical precis is a four-sentence paragraph that provides a succinct summary/analysis of a piece of writing. Writing a rhetorical precis can help students become more conscious of an author's purpose and how the author has organized and developed his/her major points to achieve that purpose.

### THE RHETORICAL PRECIS FORM

1. Name of author, genre (type of writing), title of work, date in parentheses; a rhetorically accurate verb such as "asserts," "argues," "suggests," etc.; and a THAT clause containing the major assertion (thesis statement) of the work

2. An explanation of how the author develops and/or supports the thesis, usually in chronological order

3. A statement of the author's purpose, followed by an "in order" phrase

4. A description of the intended audience and/or the relationship the author establishes with the audience

### SAMPLE

Russell Baker, in his essay, "The Art of Eating Spaghetti" (1992), reveals that he began to take himself seriously as a writer when he wrote an informal essay for his own pleasure and was praised for it. Baker develops his narrative by demonstrating how he had been bored by high school English, showing how particularly uninspiring the dreaded Mr. Fleagle had been, and how writing assignments had never interested him until he wrote from a vivid memory of learning to eat spaghetti and was praised for the essay. His purposes are to show readers how he began to take himself seriously as a writer and to reveal the connection between personal experience and self-expression. He establishes an informal relationship with the readers of *Growing Up*, his autobiography.

## THE RHETORICAL SITUATION

In 1301 and 1302, you will encounter many different types of texts, from newspaper editorials, commercials, and print advertisements to peer-reviewed journal articles, short stories, and poems. Your instructor(s) may ask you to summarize, respond to, analyze, and/or evaluate these texts in the form of an essay. To do so effectively, you will need to learn a few things about the author of the text, the audience to whom it is being addressed, the kind of text with which you are dealing, and its context. These concerns make up the rhetorical situation.

- **Author:** Whether the author is a writer, painter, singer, debater, and so on, you need to know what motivated the author to produce the text you are studying, what the author's purpose is, and what the author's attitude toward the subject of the text is. Understanding the author helps you to establish his or her *ethos*.

- **Audience:** Authors produce texts that are aimed at particular audiences. You need to know the demographics and background of a targeted audience, as well as their attitude toward the subject of the text, for that determines how the author addresses them. For example, an author may approach a hostile audience differently than a neutral audience.

- **Text:** The texts that authors produce come in a variety of forms. You need to know how those forms are created and what "rules" govern the creation of those forms. For example, the author of a newspaper editorial does not have to meet the same stringent research/scholarship requirements that the author of an academic journal article does.

- **Context:** The interaction between the author and the audience through the text occurs in a particular setting or environment. You need to know everything you can about the environment in which a text is produced, such as time, place, and any relevant social and political factors. For example, an article on border security that was published after 9/11 would be considerably different from one published in 1950.

## GROUP ASSIGNMENT: ESTABLISHING THE RHETORICAL SITUATION

Instructions: Find an editorial column, preferably with an identified author in a major newspaper. Then, going through each part of the rhetorical situation listed below, list as much information as you can.

- Author:

- Audience:

- Text:

- Context:

---

# WHAT IS RHETORICAL ANALYSIS?

There is a scene in *The Wizard of Oz* that encapsulates the idea of rhetorical analysis. Once Dorothy and crew finally reach the wizard, they enter a dark room where a giant head yells at them with a booming voice accompanied by bursts of fire. As intended, it scares them all except for Toto who runs around and finds a man pulling gizmos and gadgets behind a curtain. At this point, the head booms, "PAY NO ATTENTION TO THE MAN BEHIND THE CURTAIN!" Of course, Dorothy soon realizes that the little man behind the curtain is controlling the giant head and its booming voice. He is the wizard. Analyzing rhetoric is like discovering the man behind the curtain.

## RHETORIC

Rhetoric is any kind of text that attempts to make a point. It can be an essay like the one by Jonathan Swift arguing that Irish children should be eaten in order to solve the country's poverty problem. It can be a story like Shirley Jackson's tale about the dangers of traditions and mob mentality. But rhetoric can also be a billboard that reminds people about the pleasures of a cold drink, or it can be a commercial, a speech, or even a sketch on *Saturday Night Live*. Anything that attempts to make a point can be construed as rhetoric, and anything that can be called rhetoric can be analyzed rhetorically.

## RHETORICAL ANALYSIS

Rhetorical analysis is looking at the way a text is put together in its attempt to persuade an intended audience. Of course, in order to analyze something rhetorically, you first need to analyze its intended audience. Gender, race, age, socioeconomics, geographic region and many other factors all affect the audience's values. Our values affect why we choose to read something and how we read it, so audience is key. A text will only persuade if it taps into the values of the audience.

If you were to rhetorically analyze an essay in *Sports* magazine, you would want to think about what type of person buys this magazine and reads it. That's the intended audience. With that in mind, let's say the essay you're analyzing is about why sports are the downfall of modern society. Obviously, it is probably not going to be rhetorically effective unless it is sarcastic and not necessarily meant to be taken seriously. Why? Because the intended audience obviously values sports. To be effective, an essay has to target the audience's values.

### KAIROS

Once you figure out who the intended audience is and what their values are, the next question to ask in rhetorical analysis is, "Has the writer chosen a good time to say this?" Let's say that for some reason a number of dog attacks have taken place recently in your community, and you are analyzing a letter to the editor in today's local paper about how the city needs to do something about dog attacks. If there have been a number of dog attacks within the last few weeks in a community, a good time to say that something should be done about dog attacks is now. Waiting another couple of months may weaken the argument because the number of attacks may go down, and people won't be as concerned. What we're talking about here is the timing of the issue, which is called *kairos*. And in this case, the *kairos* would be effective because the letter writer chose to say something when the issue was hot, so the letter, however effective it is overall, has at least one thing going for it: *kairos*.

### ETHOS

Beyond timing the argument, what can writers do within a text to persuade an audience? Writers have three appeals at their disposal: *ethos*, *pathos*, and *logos*. The first appeal, *ethos*, deals with the way the writer comes across to the reader. Is the writer fair-minded in her argument? Does she seem to understand all the different sides of an issue? If so, she uses *ethos* effectively.

Another way to use *ethos* is to show that you know what you are talking about. Making grammar errors, spelling words incorrectly, and using slang can negatively affect your *ethos* depending on the audience and situation. If you are working for a large company and are typing an "everyone" email that even your supervisors will see, it's best to edit carefully before sending it; otherwise, whatever you say will be compromised by any errors you make in trying to say it, and your poor *ethos* will make for a poor email. Thus, if you are analyzing a formal essay, and it has grammar problems or slang, you would argue that the author's *ethos* is compromised, and this could have a major effect on the whole essay. Again, it depends on the intended audience.

Using sources can also affect *ethos*. Sources that readers respect boost an author's *ethos*. Conversely, if the essay you are analyzing has sources that the intended audience won't respect, then the *ethos* is negatively impacted, most likely in a major way. For example, if you are analyzing a work of literary criticism about Shakespeare's *Othello*, and the author cites *Cliff's Notes* as a source, you would find the writer's *ethos* sorely lacking because obviously the writer cut corners, which isn't respected in the world of literary critics. The primary reason a writer uses sources is to boost his *ethos*, to gain the reader's respect. This is why *Wikipedia* can actually hurt a paper, and *Google* isn't always the best place to do research.

## LOGOS

The second appeal is *logos*, which is the appeal to the reader's sense of logic. Using reasons and evidence that the audience will appreciate makes for good *logos*. Again, audience is key. Writers can't just use whatever reasons and evidence they like; they have to choose reasons and evidence they think their audience will like. For example, if you are analyzing an essay from *Family* magazine, and it argues that watching TV is a good way to spend time with the whole family because children love *Sex and the City* reruns, you would find the *logos* severely lacking. The intended audience (readers of *Family* magazine) wouldn't find this line of reasoning logical at all. The reasons have to be logically acceptable to the intended audience, or the *logos* falls apart.

## PATHOS

*Pathos* is another important appeal. This is the appeal to the readers' emotions and values, and it can make or break an argument depending on the writer's sense of audience. Diction (word choice) can affect the *pathos* of an argument. If you are analyzing an essay found in *Humanity* magazine, and the essay argues that homeless shelters need to be shut down, you know because of the intended audience (people who are interested in helping others) that the essay has a big hill to climb. Let's say the author uses the word *bum* instead of *homeless person*. Will that strike a positive chord emotionally with the intended audience? Not likely. In fact, emotionally it will probably distance the writer from the audience, so in rhetorically analyzing the essay, you would find that the *pathos* is compromised by this word choice instead of aided by it.

A writer can appeal to basically any emotion: sympathy, anger, humor, etc. In fact, humor can be a highly effective means of getting the audience on the writer's side. Super Bowl commercials are full of this kind of *pathos*, which is obviously extremely effective. As with any emotional appeal, humor can backfire, too, though. The writer must know the audience's values in order to understand what kind of emotion will work in the situation. If the audience is hostile to the writer's position, humor might be a good tool; however, humor at the audience's expense probably isn't a good idea.

As you can see, there are a number of things to look for when analyzing something rhetorically, but it all starts with the audience. Here are some rhetorical mistakes students have made in college writing by not thinking about their audience. See if you can discern why they were mistakes and what rhetorical appeals are compromised because of them.

1. Using *Spark Notes*, *FreeEssays.com*, or *Cliff's Notes* as sources

2. Using *Wikipedia* as an academic source

3. Using informal language in an academic paper

4. Failing to edit a paper carefully

5. Titling an essay "Final Draft" or "Rhetorical Analysis"

6. Using a dictionary to define a common term

7. Using first person pronouns in an academic essay

8. Plagiarizing

9. Listing supporting evidence but failing to discuss it

10. Summarizing a story instead of analyzing it

11. Revealing the ending of a movie in a movie review

---

# IDENTIFYING RHETORICAL APPEALS IN WRITTEN AND VISUAL ARGUMENTS

## PATHOS

Effective strategies for appealing to emotion and values include the following:

- concrete descriptions
- figurative language
- emotional examples and images
- values-based evidence*
- eye-catching graphics and compositional arrangement
- aesthetically-pleasing props, characters, and settings

## LOGOS

Effective strategies for appealing to reason include the following:

- syllogistic logic (deductive reasoning)
- historical precedent
- expert testimony
- hard facts, statistics, studies, and reports
- charts, graphs, and tables
- discipline-specific language
- definitions
- research and critical apparatus (i.e., sources)
- clear thesis-support structures and transitions
- discussion of evidence

## ETHOS

Effective strategies for appealing to character include the following:

- strong *pathos* and *logos*
- appropriate style (tone of voice and diction)
- non-confrontational rhetoric
- correct grammar, mechanics, and documentation
- accurate and contextualized quotations and paraphrases
- fair treatment and representation of other viewpoints
- endorsements and brand-name recognition
- qualified positions
- credentials

---

*Values: convenience, class, freedom, safety, elitism, simplicity, efficiency, cost, morality, fear, sex, family, love, community, fitness, trends, power, relationship, outdoors, beauty, commitment, politics, conversation, competition, hunger, race, charity, partying, lifestyle, risk taking, ethnicity, culture, adventure, progress, proximity, size

# ADVERTISEMENTS' FIFTEEN BASIC EMOTIONAL APPEALS

"The continuous pressure is to create ads more and more in the image of audience motives and desires." – Marshall McLuhan, *Understanding Media*

Advertisements can appeal to:

1. The need for sex
2. The need for affiliation
3. The need to nurture
4. The need for guidance
5. The need to aggress
6. The need to achieve
7. The need to dominate
8. The need for prominence
9. The need for attention
10. The need for autonomy
11. The need to escape
12. The need to feel safe
13. The need for aesthetic sensations
14. The need to satisfy curiosity
15. Physiological needs: food, drink, sleep, etc.

Excerpt from Jib Fowles's "Advertising's Fifteen Basic Appeals" in *Common Culture: Reading and Writing About American Popular Culture*. Ed. Michael Petracca and Madeleine Sorapure. Upper Saddle River: Prentice, 1998. Print.

# GENERAL RUBRIC FOR ENGLISH 1301 AND 1302 PAPERS

| Criterion | F 0% | D 65% | C 75% | B 85% | A 95% | A+ 100% | Total |
|---|---|---|---|---|---|---|---|
| **Requirements 20%** Specific assignment requirements including (but not limited to) length, format, MLA documentation, required sources, response to prompt, academic register, third person prose | **0 points** even if most requirements are met, a paper without sources and/or quotations automaticlly fails | **13 points** one or two requirements not met | **15 points** all requirements met but in a safe and stilted way | **17 points** all requirements met | **19 points** engagement with the prompt is original and refreshing, demonstrating intelligence and discernment | **20 points** | 20 |
| **Introduction 5%** Engages the audience, frames the issue, leads up to thesis | **0 points** no introduction provided; probably begins with the thesis | **3.25 points** intro not too much general, often relying on generic or obvious statements; does not engage audience at all | **3.75 points** intro is a bit safe and possibly too short, but there is an attempt to engage the audience | **4.25 points** generates interesting context and sets up the thesis well | **4.75 points** compelling and captivating; builds up to thesis well; nice balance of general and specific | **5 points** | 5 |
| **Thesis 5%** The explicit position statement the paper will defend | **0 points** no thesis evident | **3.25 points** thesis may be implied but is not immediately apparent | **3.75 points** thesis is present but may be poorly framed or lacking tension | **4.25 points** good focus; enough tension to sustain interest | **4.75 points** thesis is sophisticated, challenging, and exciting | **5 points** | 5 |
| **Support 25%** Topic sentences that seek to prove the thesis statement; relevant evidence, from primary and secondary sources, that backs up topic sentences, and explanations that tie the evidence to topic sentences and thesis statement | **0 points** no support provided | **16.25 points** discussions and examples are confusing and underdeveloped: reasons are not entirely supportive and/or evidence is not sufficiently discussed and tied to thesis | **18.75 points** some problems with development, specifically tying evidence to thesis, but argument has sufficient support to cause the reader to consider it | **21.25 points** support is relevant and connected to the thesis; evidence is explained in a convincing way | **23.75 points** support is sophisticated, relevant, nuanced, and sufficiently exhaustive | **25 points** | 25 |
| **Organization 10%** Arrangement of reasons and logical development of argument as well as unity and coherence of paragraphs with transitions | **0 points** paper is incoherent | **6.5 points** some focus, but paragraphs are not connected in a logical way, and transitions are virtually nonexistent | **7.5 points** mostly clear progression with one or two digressions, yet mechanically sequential rather than sophisticated and logical | **8.5 points** connections of all elements are evident and logically consistent, presenting few problems for the reader to follow the argument's development | **9.5 points** organization is seamless, clearly enhancing the argument | **10 points** | 10 |

| Criterion | F 0% | D 65% | C 75% | B 85% | A 95% | A+ 100% | Total |
|---|---|---|---|---|---|---|---|
| **Documentation 10%** Correctness and accuracy of in-text citations and works-cited page | **0 points** pervasive problems with misdocumented and/or undocumented plagiarism | **6.5 points** some problems with misdocumented plagiarism | **7.5 points** no problems with either type of plagiarism, but a number of citations in-text and on the works-cited page are inaccurate, incomplete, and/or improperly formatted | **8.5 points** some minor problems with in-text citations and the works-cited page | **9.5 points** one or two minor problems | **10 points** | 10 |
| **Style 10%** Diction, sentence variety, tone appropriate for purpose and audience | **0 points** inappropriate for audience due to offensive and/or controversial language | **6.5 points** conversational tone; frequently relies on first and/or second person pronouns | **7.5 points** conversational at times with an overall effort to present an academic tone | **8.5 points** no lapses into first or second person, but some problems with sentence variety and tone | **9.5 points** convincingly academic with fluid sentences sparked with variety and rich, vivid language | **10 points** | 10 |
| **Grammar 10%** Sentence-level errors including (but not limited to) fragments, run-ons, shifts, misspellings, and typos | **0 points** grammar errors that seriously weaken the writer's ethos (see instructor for help with editing) | **6.5 points** grammar errors begin to hoard the reader's attention | **7.5 points** an attempt to control grammar errors; a few problems which may reflect editing issues instead of conceptual problems | **8.5 points** a few mistakes, but overall an admirable job of editing | **9.5 points** near perfect sentence-level control | **10 points** | 10 |
| **Conclusion 5%** | **0 points** no conclusion provided | **3.25 points** conclusion merely restates the thesis | **3.75 points** conclusion moves beyond simply restating the argument, but does not engage the audience sufficiently | **4.25 points** conclusion attempts to address the significance of argument and engage the audience's interest | **4.75 points** presentation of the conclusion leaves the audience considering the argument long after reading the paper | **5 points** | 5 |
| **TOTAL:** | | | | | | | 100 |

# English
# 1301

# THE BASIC STRUCTURE OF AN ESSAY

The essays students write in Freshman Composition I will be between 500–800 words and will usually consist of 4–6 paragraphs. Students will write different types of essays, and each type will have special characteristics. However, all essays should contain the following components:

## INTRODUCTION

You must always introduce your subject matter. The purpose of an introduction is to orient your reader, providing him/her with necessary background information so that the rest of your essay can be understood. For example, if you are writing an argument essay against active euthanasia, you should define this term for your reader and explain the nature of the controversy before presenting your stand. In most essays, the introduction should contain your THESIS STATEMENT, often as the last sentence.

## THESIS STATEMENT

Your thesis statement asserts the opinion or idea that you will support in your essay. The thesis is usually expressed in one sentence. The thesis reveals to the reader what you will be covering in your essay and also helps you stay focused. An essay of 500-800 words cannot adequately develop and support more than one central idea, so your thesis should not attempt to accomplish too much. An example of an effective thesis statement for a descriptive essay is "My Aunt Leanne is a flashy extrovert." An example of an ineffective thesis statement is "My aunts and uncles tend to be extroverted" or "My Aunt Leanne is extroverted and shouldn't believe in capital punishment." Both of these thesis statements have more than one central idea. It would not be possible to describe adequately all aunts and uncles in one essay, and arguments against the capital punishment constitute a separate task requiring another essay.

Although a thesis contains one central idea, this idea has different components or parts which can be spelled out in the thesis statement itself. In the sample thesis, "My Aunt Leanne is a flashy extrovert," there are two components—that she has a flashy appearance and that she has an extroverted personality. These components are often called the thesis points, which should be supported in the body paragraphs. It is not necessary to spell out your thesis points in the thesis. For example, you might use the thesis "Capital punishment should remain legal" without spelling out the points you will cover to defend that opinion. Whether or not you spell out your points in the thesis, you must make sure that your body paragraphs support your thesis.

## BODY PARAGRAPHS

Your essay will contain from 2–4 paragraphs in the body of your essay—appearing after the introduction and before the conclusion. Each body paragraph should support an aspect of your thesis or a specific thesis point. This aspect or thesis point is revealed in the first sentence of the body paragraph—the TOPIC SENTENCE. The remaining sentences in the paragraph should develop and support the topic sentence. If you are writing about your flashy, extroverted Aunt Leanne, your first body paragraph might look something like this:

### SAMPLE

Aunt Leanne has always been a flashy dresser. She prefers to wear flowing caftans of bright red or purple, her favorite colors. She also wears quite a bit of jewelry, usually multi-colored bracelets and painted dangle earrings. Her makeup is hardly understated, as she typically wears more than one coat of pancake foundation, fire engine-red lipstick, and sparkly blue or purple eyeshadow. Sometimes all this red clashes oddly with her orange hair, which she wears in a much-teased beehive. We have never seen Aunt Leanne in black or grey, even at funerals.

Notice how all the supporting sentences after the topic sentence provide details and examples about her flashy appearance.

The next body paragraph might go on to describe her extroverted personality. A well-developed paragraph should have at least five sentences. If the paragraph above had only three sentences, we probably would not get a complete "picture" of Aunt Leanne's flashy appearance.

## CONCLUSION

Your conclusion should be the last paragraph in your essay. An effective conclusion does not simply restate all the points made—nor does it introduce any new ideas. A good conclusion reinforces your main idea. There are several methods you can use to reinforce your message, including ending with an apt quotation or a provocative thought that causes your readers to consider some new implications concerning your topic. In concluding your essay about your Aunt Leanne, you might say something like this:

### SAMPLE

Because of her flashy, extroverted nature, Aunt Leanne is often perceived as a shallow attention seeker. However, those who know her best realize that her need to connect with other people is inspired not by selfishness, but by a sincere love of people. She has friends from around the world and sends them cards and presents on their birthdays. As she has often said, "Some see a stranger, but I see a new friend waiting to happen."

# WHAT CAN I PUT IN MY THREE-PART ESSAY?

These suggestions are optional. Not all strategies work equally well for all essays. Think of this list as a buffet, and choose the techniques that work best for the assignment and the rhetorical situation.

## I. INTRODUCTION

A. Anecdote (if approved by the instructor)

B. Startling statement (attention-grabber)

C. Dramatic fact or statistic

D. Question (or a short series of questions)

E. Idea that is the opposite of the one you actually develop ("Many people think that...but...")

F. Background

G. Examples

H. Broad statement that narrows to a limited subject

I. Thesis statement

## II. BODY

A. Examples

B. Details

C. Facts or statistics

D. Quotations, especially expert opinions

E. Lists

F. Definition

G. Reasons

H. Comparison-contrast

I. Description

J. Dialogue (if approved by instructor)

K. Narration (if approved by instructor)

L. Division-classification (analysis)

M. Before and after

N. Process (how something is done)

O. Cause-effect (why something is the way it is or what the result will be)

## III. CONCLUSION

A. Summary (Summaries work best for long essays; for five-, six-, or seven-paragraph essays, try another method.)

B. Restatement of thesis

C. Answer the question raised in the introduction

D. Quotation

E. Anecdote (if allowed by instructor)

F. Prediction

G. Fact or statistic

H. Recommendation or call to action (Beware of shifting to the second person with this strategy.)

I. "So what" factor. Explain the significance of the topic.

---

## JOURNAL WRITING

Many instructors require students to keep journals. Journal entries may be observations about personal experiences or observations of world or local events. Letting ideas flow to a page may be considered as a form of free writing with organization.

Many professionals will say that journal writing is healthy. It provides a form of therapy by allowing a person to shape thoughts and process experiences from the past. It allows a person the opportunity to gain insight by organizing and rearranging thoughts as one can do in an essay.

When a person faces a problem, journal writing gives the individual the occasion to develop clarity with organizing thoughts, both pro and con, to gain a better perspective of a situation.

The reasons for journal writing may vary, but the desired outcomes are often the same: practice, practice, and more practice of putting pen-to-paper, or in more recent years, words-to-word processor; but in either case, the student has an opportunity to put thoughts-to-page. This allows students to become more expressive and more organized when they need to write details in an essay.

Students may be given one topic to write about, they may be given a list from which to select, or they may be assigned free writing over any topic they might choose. In any case, the lubrication of using the mind to express oneself in an organized manner is beneficial in the overall writing process. Write. Write. Write.

# DESCRIPTIVE WRITING

Description is writing that creates an image using words. You use sensory details—touch, smell, sight, taste, and sound—to generate an image in the reader's mind. Descriptive writing has sentences and paragraphs that work together to present a single, clear picture (description) of a person, a place, a thing, an event, or an idea.

When you write description, you will select the supporting details and words that will most effectively communicate one single *dominant impression* of the subject. This dominant impression becomes the topic sentence of the paragraph or the thesis statement of an essay. It also guides your choice of details to be included in the paper.

Organize your writing in a method (space, time, themes, or logic) which will fit your topic and your purpose. Descriptive writing is often arranged in a spatial organization. You might describe an object from top to bottom or a room from left to right. You would arrange your sentences and details to describe the way something looks, sounds, tastes, feels, or smells. You can also use chronological organization. You might describe a rafting trip from when you pushed your raft into the river all the way through to when you pulled your raft out of the river. In between, you would add sensory details of the trip as they happened. The type of organization you choose should be relevant to your topic and purpose of your writing.

Descriptive writing can also be objective or subjective. Objective description relies on observable details and facts. It avoids emotional details and subjective emotions. Subjective description can include your thoughts, feelings, and moods. Subjective descriptions can create powerful impressions. Writers often blend the two. By blending subjective and objective descriptions, you can use both logical and emotional appeals. You can present factual information with emotional impressions.

Remember:

- The purpose of description is to help the reader visualize what you are describing.

- The writing should have one dominant impression that is clear to the reader.

- It should include sensory details using as many of the five senses as possible.

- It should use an organization that fits the topic and purpose of the paper.

## NARRATIVE WRITING

One type of narrative writing is telling a fictional story. Another type, which is most commonly assigned in composition classes, is telling a story that actually happened by depicting a sequence of related events. Effective narratives include specific details and descriptions that help the reader follow the events and visualize the story.

The story in the narrative can be about you, someone you know, or an event in history. The main idea of the story (thesis or topic sentence) will tell the reader why you are telling the story. Make sure the main point states the goal of the narrative and what you want your readers to understand from the story. Clarifying your purpose will help you to select which details to add to your paper.

Narration is usually told in straight chronological order. You will want to choose events that pertain to your story and write those events in the order that they occurred. Before beginning your paper, you might find it helpful to write a timeline of the events of your story. This could help organize your material chronologically, include all your events, and put them into the correct order before incorporating them in your paper.

You can use transitional words and phrases as you arrange the events of your narrative. These words and phrases help the reader follow the plot of your story. Some of these words include: first, second, then after, by the time, and later on.

You can write your narrative in first or third person. If the story is about you, then you will probably want to use first person (I, me, mine, we). If the subject of your story is another person or an event in history, you might want to use third person (he, she, they, John, Marsha).

In the conclusion, you should come to an important point about the narrative that you just described. The conclusion will finalize your essay. You want to make sure that the reader understands the point of the narrative. You can end your conclusion by reflecting on the larger meaning or the importance of the experience described.

Remember:

- The thesis statement or topic sentence of a narrative relates the main idea of the story and tells the reader why you are telling the story.

- The story is usually told in straight time (chronological) order.

- Relevant events are included to flesh out the story.

- The narrative ends by reminding the reader of the purpose of the story.

# THE COMPARISON/CONTRAST ESSAY

A comparison/contrast essay explains the similarities or differences between two subjects. We use comparison/contrast thinking when we decide which college to attend or which car to buy. For example, when we compare colleges, we might consider each college's location, tuition cost, and curriculum. A comparison/contrast essay should have a <u>purpose</u>—what you intend to demonstrate through comparing or contrasting two subjects. The purpose of a comparison/contrast essay might be to <u>clear up confusion</u> or create clear distinctions between two similar subjects. For example, you could explain the differences between two types of laptops or two social networking sites to help readers become informed. You might also want to express a <u>preference</u>, to explain why you prefer one restaurant over another or one band over another, for example. It could also be interesting to demonstrate that two seemingly <u>unlike</u> subjects actually have some things in common. For example, you could show that two politicians from opposing parties actually share some traits and interests. You could also demonstrate that two seemingly <u>similar</u> subjects are actually quite different. For example, you could explain how two siblings do not look anything alike and have different personalities.

Once you choose your comparison/contrast topic and your purpose, you should choose either a <u>subject-by-subject</u> or <u>point-by-point</u> method of organization. A subject-by-subject method examines one subject at a time, while a point-by-point method examines one point of comparison at a time. In either method, you need to be sure to use the <u>same points of comparison</u> when examining the two subjects.

The sample outlines below illustrate these two methods of organization.

SAMPLE

Subject-By-Subject

I. Thesis: I prefer Tony's Italian Kitchen to Joe's Pizzeria because Tony's Italian Kitchen has more menu options, a nicer atmosphere, and more reasonable prices.

II. Joe's Pizzeria

A. Limited menu options

B. Noisy atmosphere

C. Inflated prices

III. Tony's Italian Kitchen

A. Variety of menu options

B. Charming atmosphere

C. Reasonable prices

Point-By-Point

I.  Thesis: I prefer Tony's Italian Kitchen to Joe's Pizzeria because Tony's Italian Kitchen has more menu options, a nicer atmosphere, and more reasonable prices.

II.  Menu Options

   A. Joe's Pizzeria's limited menu options

   B. Tony's Italian Kitchen's variety of menu options

III.  Atmosphere

   A. Joe's Pizzeria's noisy atmosphere

   B. Tony's Italian Kitchen's charming atmosphere

IV.  Prices

   A. Joe's Pizzeria's inflated prices

   B. Tony's Italian Kitchen's reasonable prices

## THE VISUAL ANALYSIS ESSAY

Those of you who have been assigned a visual analysis essay will benefit from the following sample essay. Rhetorically analyzing an advertisement for the Wendy's Baconator, the essay features

- a functional, yet clever title

- an opening that establishes a cultural and historical context

- an explicit thesis statement that clearly announces whether the ad being analyzed is effective in reaching its target audience

- a paragraph of thick description of what is going on in the ad

- body paragraphs with topic sentences that extend and develop the thesis and specify the rhetorical appeal being addressed

- a conclusion that does not merely restate the thesis

What it does not provide, however, are fully developed body paragraphs, yet listed beneath each topic sentence is evidence from the ad that would be used to support each topic sentence. The outlined presentation, moreover, should help you to see the parts of a visual analysis essay and how the argument flows from the thesis. When drafting your essay, you should consider using an outline like this one.

## VISUAL ANALYSIS OF WENDY'S BACONATOR AD

### I. Introductory Section

**Title:** Double Meat, Double Cheese, Extra Pathos, Please: A High-Calorie Rhetorical Analysis of "The New Baconator"

**Opening Remarks:** A recent trend in the last five years, within the fast-food industry, is a concerted push toward more health-conscious options. McDonald's, the king of fast food, now offers fruit cups and granola. Burger King and Jack-in-the-Box list veggie burgers on their menus. Soon, the entire fast-food industry will cave to an inordinate amount of pressure from salad-eating, fruit-juice drinking, soy-conscious dieticians, posing as parents, who condemn anyone who would dare consider buttering his or her bacon (which is the only legitimate way to eat bacon).

In the midst of this pressure, however, a few fast-food restaurants have not completely conformed; one, in fact, hurls grease at the iron-depleted visage of the enemy and has proclaimed, "Top your meat with meat; garnish with cheese; hold the pansy." Wendy's once again, in an ad for "The New Baconator," has thumbed its nose at caloric and cholesterol intake.

**Thesis Statement:** This ad effectively persuades its target audience, which consists of consumers who love fast food and can't get enough of it.

**Summary Paragraph:** Presented as a movie poster, the ad for "The New Baconator" is over-the-top, much like a bloated sequel should be. True to form, the ad immediately catches the eye with the product itself, sitting boldly on a background of red. The burger occupies nearly half of the total space in the ad and for good reason: two patties, two pieces of cheese, and six strips of bacon, not to mention the fluffy cloud-like bun that gently rests on a veritable pallet of goodness. To enhance the visual image, the ad provides a wonderfully vivid description of the burger and makes use of a theatrical vernacular to present its powerful claim: "Try it if you dare."

### II. Main Body Section

**1. *Ethos:*** After the sheer size of the burger captivates its famished audience, the familiarity of the brand and other elements of ethos pull them in and keep their interest the way a good actor brings in an audience to a mediocre movie.

    a.   brand-name recognition

    b.   cultural status of Wendy's

    c.   "Fresh, never frozen"

**2. *Logos:*** Even a famished audience, however, requires strong reasons to spend money on one food product instead of another, which is why the Wendy's ad utilizes visual effects and copy text to appeal to logic.

    a.   size of burger on page

    b.   detailed description of burger specifications

    c.   combo options

**3. *Pathos:*** Backing up its logos, the Wendy's ad then adds layer after layer of pathos to appeal to its audience's attitude toward food and insatiable appetite.

    a.   personification of burger

    b.   theatrical and combative rhetoric

    c.   appearance

*III. Conclusion*

Although America did not invent the buffet, it surely perfected it and made overeating glamorous besides. In a land of plenty, where one may be a hero for consuming fifteen pounds of duck liver in five minutes, the new Wendy's ad is a testament to all that America stands for, in addition to freedom—but served up with a side of patriotism.

---

# THE RHETORICAL ANALYSIS ESSAY

The following essay is a rhetorical analysis of Rick Reilly's "Bare in Mind."[1] In the essay, the writer argues that Reilly's article is an effective piece of writing by closely examining his use of rhetorical appeals—such as *pathos, logos,* and *ethos*—in targeting his audience. As you read it, please note the following:

- The introduction establishes a context for understanding the impact of Reilly's work and leads into an explicit thesis statement.

- The thesis statement clearly announces the writer's position on Reilly's rhetorical decisions and provides an enumerated plan for the rest of the essay.

- Each topic sentence follows logically from the thesis and deals with one of the rhetorical appeals.

- The writer includes enough evidence from the article in the form of quotations and summary.

The sample essay below is by no means perfect, and certainly you should consider whether it effectively analyzes Reilly's article (a rhetorical analysis of a rhetorical analysis!). A sample essay like this one, however, will help with your analyses of written arguments, especially if your instructor has assigned you something similar.

### *Topless: Exposing Rick Reilly's Use of Rhetoric in "Bare in Mind"*[2]

ESPN revolutionized sports news in 1979 when it launched a 24/7 cable news network featuring Sports Center, the anchors of which have landed film roles, late night talk shows, and other significant entertainment gigs because of ESPN's overwhelming success. ESPN would not have been possible, however, without the success of *Sports*

---

[1]  The article is available at http://sportsillustrated.cnn.com/vault/article/magazine/MAG1020254/index.htm

[2]  *Sports Illustrated* Magazine. *Echo Media.* Echo Media, 2008. Web. 21 May 2008.

*Illustrated*. Since 1954 *SI* has fed the public's need for complete and extensive coverage of the world of sports by writers at the top of their game. With an annual circulation over 160,000,000 ("*Sports Illustrated* Magazine"), *SI* has solidified itself as the most important and popular sports magazine, which like ESPN is largely responsible for shaping attitudes toward sports, athletes, and the issues that affect both. Its audience primarily consists of men (over 70%) with an average age of 37 and income over $60,000 ("*Sports Illustrated* Magazine"), who often cite the magazine's writers as the main reason they subscribe—well, after the swimsuit edition.

Senior writer Rick Reilly, whose "Life of Reilly" column was a fixture in *SI* for years, is well aware of this audience and attuned to their political, social, and cultural viewpoints. As such, he typically puts forth provocative opinions designed to entertain the masses but irritate others. For some, he is the rhetorical equivalent of BENGAY in a jockstrap. **In "Bare in Mind," an article responding to the outrage a seminude photo of Jenny Thompson garnered, Reilly effectively presents his position by appealing to values he and his audience share, by using an entertaining rebuttal style his audience would appreciate, and by incorporating just enough evidence to lend credence to a viewpoint his audience probably shares.**

Reilly knows that his audience values sports and all things related to sports, including fitness, desire, commitment, and self-confidence. Reilly's initial goal, therefore, is to focus on how each of those is evident in Thompson's photo. Attempting to divert attention away from whatever sex might be in that photo, Reilly cites Thompson's developed physique: her "[k]iller thighs that could crush anvils" and "[c]alves sharp enough to slice [a] tomato." The photo, in other words, is not about sex, according to Reilly, but is a testament to her work ethic. Indeed, Reilly argues that Thompson's motivation to bare all stems from "[spending] her whole life looking at the bottom of swimming pools. If she had to miss a lifetime of proms and parties and triple fudge cake, at least she should be able to show the world what she was building in the gym six hours a day." Reilly understands that his audience will be able to appreciate Thompson's sacrifices because of their interest in sports and the likelihood that they have participated in sports at some amateur level. Pointing out her sacrifices, in fact, allows Reilly to shift whatever disapproval his audience may have toward the photo to something positive.

What makes this diversionary tactic so impressive, though, is how he exploits and subverts the arguments made by the "hypocrites." To illustrate to his audience the hypocrisy of the letter writers, Reilly employs an engaging and entertaining style that sustains interest while simultaneously destroying the opposition. For example, he uses a bit of misdirection at the start to draw a distinction between a viewer who sees only sex and one who sees athleticism:

> Wow, Jenny Thompson has a nice pair, doesn't she? Massive. Firm. Perfectly shaped.
>
> Her thighs, I mean.

Most readers would expect him to have written "breasts" instead, which is why "thighs" both startles the reader and then draws attention to a positive feature in a joking way.

(And this needling approach nicely demonstrates to those who find sex in the photo that it does not have to be about sex.) Such humor is important to his audience. A dry, academic refutation would quickly lose interest, but a true sports fan would keep reading Reilly's article because of its sarcastic, occasionally caustic tone.

Also, he points out that the "hypocrites" who claim to value freedom and liberation are actually denying a consequence or symptom of such freedom. Reilly, talking about other female athletes who have posed in the nude, argues,

> These women aren't hung up about getting liberated. They *are* liberated, were born that way. They're coming from a whole new place in feminism—rugged, gorgeous, prideful athleticism—free of the old, butch, male-hater stereotype women jocks used to fight.

Reilly's audience would respond to this passage in particular because he suggests that they are more liberated than the "hypocrites." In fact, by contrast those who find sex in the photo are, according to Reilly, perpetuating other stereotypes. It is a brilliant move that connects Reilly with his readers, who now can confidently say about themselves that they are more liberated in their attitudes about women than the very women who wrote in and complained. What male sports fan would not be able to appreciate the biting humor in that role reversal?

While his audience will certainly be entertained by his wit, they will also appreciate the actual evidence he uses. He points out that male athletes also pose in the nude, thus demonstrating that there appears to be a double standard if the female athletes who pose in the nude are the only targets of outrage. Additionally, Reilly reasons that ultimately people should applaud women like Thompson who have "*real* bodies, *fit* bodies, *attainable* bodies—not bodies you can only get through the Lucky Gene Club or plastic surgery or throwing up your lunch every day." His readers at this point would understand the larger context—concerning unhealthy body images, the prevalence of eating disorders, etc.—and make the connection that Thompson's photo might actually be helpful. Finally, the historical analogy Reilly ends with firmly establishes his position with his audience. He asks, "And will somebody please remind de Varona that ancient Olympians competed in the nude in the first place?" In other words, nudity and sports are not mutually opposed, and a significant historical precedent exists. On the other hand, modern Olympians would be wise to keep their clothes on, especially male hurdlers.

Had Reilly written this piece for, say, *Redbook*, he would have been more restrained and comprehensive with his argument. But for his *SI* audience the article works because of his rhetorical decisions about how to incorporate *pathos* and *logos*. He identifies values important to his audience, approaches them in an engaging manner, and provides them with enough evidence to make his article slightly more serious. And for those who still disagree with his position, perhaps they might appreciate his ability to write for an audience.

### Works Cited

Reilly, Rick. "Bare in Mind." *SI.com.* Time Warner, 4 Sept. 2000. Web. 21 May 2008.

"*Sports Illustrated Magazine.*" *Echo Media.* Echo Media, 2008. Web. 21 May 2008.

# PROPOSAL PAPER

Pretend for the moment that you work for AmeriTube, a company that specializes in athletic tube socks. Every week, the marketing department has a meeting in which the advertisers present new marketing ideas and ad campaigns to promote AmeriTube's product line, especially its best-known product, "The Über-Tube," a knee-high sock that promotes circulation.

The problem, however, is that the department has ten marketers who each present a new idea during the meeting time. You, a member of upper-management, have to listen to each new idea and consult afterward with the upper-management team to determine which ideas are viable and which are not.

Well, these meetings, you have noticed, tend to drag on for more than two hours because the marketers go overboard with presentation materials and other types of content delivery.

Quite frankly, the weekly meetings are preventing you from accomplishing other important activities, so you decide to tell your boss that the way the meetings are conducted needs to change to make them more efficient and economical. Your boss, however, has always maintained that she likes creativity and wants to hear from all of her "creative personnel."

So you know that the meetings are too long and that time could be better spent for the company. But the meeting is for the marketers, and their ideas must be heard. What is your proposal?

    a. Provide a donut bar in the meeting with a barista on hand.

    b. Move the meetings to a hotel conference room, preferably a hotel with a pool.

    c. Fire nine of the marketers.

    d. Limit each marketer to five minutes of presentation time.

Okay, "a" is tempting, but "d" is probably the best choice. Obviously, "c" is the worst option in terms of audience, the boss.

A proposal argument is actually a familiar real-world situation. All of you have made proposals, at one time or another, in the context of family, work, or elsewhere. Daily, we encounter problems. Daily, we hear about problems. When we face a problem, what do we want to do? Find a solution—and that is precisely what a proposal argument seeks to do.

Proposal arguments do three things, and always three things. They identify and define an existing problem, evaluate any existing and proposed solutions, and then propose the best solution.

Perhaps more so in proposals than in other rhetorical modes, audience is the crucial factor. Presumably, proposals are aimed at those who can effect change—that is, if we want to change something, we target those who have the power to change. Therefore, proposal writing makes considerable demands on the writer to learn as much as possible about the target audience. Indeed, proposal writing at every level requires audience awareness, from tone of voice to audience-based reasons, from organization to possible audience objections.

When you're writing your proposal argument, here's a good outline to follow:

1. Establish the problem; convince the reader that this is not only a problem, but one that is serious and significant, worthy of efforts to solve it. Use research to establish the problem: statistics, stories of individuals affected by the problem, etc.

2. Discuss other proposed solutions that haven't worked or won't work. Be sure to argue why. Feel free to address them one at a time in separate paragraphs if needed. Use research if one of these solutions has been used before or is in place now and not working.

3. Announce your solution and the clear steps we'll need to take to implement the solution. Make sure that it is specific, not just, "We need to do a better job... ." Make sure to argue why your solution is best. If needed, address the argument against your solution and show why those who hold this belief are wrong. Don't be offensive, however. In a proposal argument, you're reaching out to those who might oppose you, not trying to shout them down.

The general pattern for developing a topic is → **Topic Issue Question** → **Thesis (Proposal) Statement.**

> **Topic:** Parking at Amarillo College
>
> **Issue Question:** What can be done to solve the problem of parking at Amarillo College?
>
> **Thesis Statement:** X will solve the problem of parking at Amarillo College.

Glossed over in this sequence, however, is actually choosing a topic. First, you need to begin with the type of assignment you have: proposal argument. Second, you need to consider what does and does not fit into proposal writing.

Proposals typically fall under two categories, practice and policy, but not every topic lends itself to the problem-solution format of a proposal. Consider the following proposal paper scenarios:

1a. The problem: Abortion is legal.

1b. The solution: Make it illegal.

2a. The problem: Capital punishment is wrong.

2b. The solution: Get rid of it.

Assuming that you are arguing 1a or 2a, your solution depends on whether people agree that the problem is in fact a problem. If some people do not view the legality of abortion as being a problem, you cannot argue your solution, and if they did agree that the legality of abortion is a problem, then they already support your solution, so what's the point of spending time arguing the solution? In other words, the problem presupposes the solution. If readers accept the problem as stated, there is no need for the writer to defend his/her solution.

You see, broad topics, particularly those that potentially have a rather divisive effect, just don't work well for a proposal paper. A good proposal topic identifies a problem that most everyone would agree (after enough evidence has been presented) is a problem. The controversy, then, comes into play regarding how serious it is (or to what degree it is a problem), whether it needs to be addressed now, and how it's going to be addressed in terms of a solution.

For example, reasonable people acknowledge that the increasing use of methamphetamine among youth is a problem. No reasonable person says, "I think more young people should use meth. And then they should drive. Fast." But reasonable people may disagree on how best to deal with meth use. You see the difference?

So the first thing to do is pick a topic that

- is narrow, focused,

- interesting to you,

- and that lends itself to rational discussion.

Obesity is a good topic. To satisfy #1, a student could focus on obesity among preteens in America. If the student is a parent, no doubt he/she would be interested in anything dealing with children and school, and more broadly with the health of the nation (#2). And finally, such a topic, while serious and important, does not carry quite the same amount of baggage that abortion does (#3).

The issue question would be: What could be done to bring down the obesity rate among preteens in America? The answer to that question, the proposal, is the thesis.

But we need to restrict further. In the solution section, we could not tackle the media, the family, and the school environment in just one paper. So we might restrict ourselves to what schools could do to address obesity, and then explore the feasibility and effectiveness of those potential solutions, such as a health curriculum, healthy cafeteria options, vending machine changes, and physical education.

One last thing to consider when writing a proposal paper is research. With whatever topic you choose, you will have to locate credible sources that provide information and support. Sometimes, research requires creative thinking.

If your topic is homelessness in Amarillo (and your issue question is *What can be done about homelessness in Amarillo?*), will you be able to find articles on homelessness in Amarillo? Sure. The *Amarillo Globe-News* will have some articles on it. But what about scholarly articles? Not likely. You will be able to find, however, a number of scholarly articles that deal with the issue of homelessness in a variety of ways. You cannot discuss homelessness in Amarillo until you understand homelessness in general.

In addition to local sources in newspapers and general sources in scholarly journals, you could conduct field research by interviewing local homeless shelter directors, people who are homeless, directors of local charities that help the homeless, and perhaps police officers.

Now, the proposal paper is one kind of argumentative research paper. For a more general discussion of argumentative research papers, go to *http://owl.english. purdue.edu*. There you will find handouts on writing a research paper, as well as other helpful material pertaining to rhetoric, composition, documentation, and grammar.

## ETHOS

Your teacher walks into class on the first day without any books or papers in hand. His hair is disheveled and matted in places with what appears to be egg salad. Bleary eyed and winded from a single flight of stairs, he readjusts his shorts and suspenders, stifles a burp, and looks up.

"What class is this? 1301? '02?" he asks.

"It's 0301, sir," says one of the students.

He scans the room, snorts, and says, "Look around. That's right. Look around. Most of you are going to fail. Welcome to 0301."

Okay, so the example is silly, but no doubt many of the students in this situation would be worried, perhaps even fearful, about whether or not they would succeed and to what extent the teacher would contribute to that.

"He doesn't want to teach this class," they might be thinking. Or "he doesn't care about us." After all, the teacher is unaware of which class he is supposed to be teaching. And if he doesn't know that information at the start, what else doesn't he know? Will he be an effective teacher? He certainly does not inspire much confidence.

The problem here, of course, is that the teacher in this situation is not coming across favorably to the students. His attire, appearance, and attitude are shaping the way they see him, and that perception more than likely will affect the way they listen to him in class as the semester progresses.

No matter in what situation you find yourself communicating to an audience—a friendly conversation, a student–teacher conference, a meeting with a potential employer, a parent–child talk, a 1301 research paper, and so on—you are creating a persona, whether you know it or not. Your attitude, nonverbal communication, attire, personal history, and presentation, for example, all may contribute to shaping the way the audience perceives you. If you are not careful about how you are coming across, the audience's perception of you can be detrimental to what you are trying to communicate. In fact, they might not trust you; and, if they do not trust you, why would they listen to you?

This is *ethos*—the way a person comes across to his or her audience in terms of credibility. In a sense, *ethos* is the most important rhetorical appeal because you cannot sell your argument if you cannot sell yourself. Think about it. Would you buy a car from a salesperson you did not trust? Probably not.

In the first-ever televised presidential debate, for example, between J. F. Kennedy and Richard Nixon in 1960, perception played an important role. Over sixty million Americans watched the debate unfold, and the general consensus is that JFK won because he looked better on the screen than the recently hospitalized and ill-looking Nixon. Interestingly, the majority of those who listened to the debate on the radio thought Nixon won. Nixon's sickly appearance did not inspire a great deal of trust next to the robust JFK, so the content of his message to the American people was less effective, less convincing.

The question for you as writers, then, is this: *What can I do and what should I avoid to establish my* ethos *as a writer?* As writers and communicators within an academic context, you may undermine or establish your *ethos* in a number of ways.

|  | **Undermine *Ethos*** | **Establish *Ethos*** |
|---|---|---|
| **Focus:** the extent to which the content of the essay corresponds to the thesis statement | A writer loses credibility when he/she fails to provide an explicit or implicit thesis. Without a thesis, an essay has no main point, so readers are left to construct the meaning and point of the essay for themselves. A weak thesis—which is vague, generic, or which lacks tension—also creates similar problems. Sometimes, a writer does provide a clear thesis. If the essay does not relate to the thesis, however, then readers still will not know what's going on in the essay. | A writer must strive for good focus, which means that the thesis statement drives the entire essay. Each section, then, focuses on presenting and arguing the thesis statement with logical reasoning, supportive evidence, and correct documentation. Good focus keeps readers in the rhetorical flow of the essay. |
| **Organization:** the order in which ideas are presented in support of the thesis statement | A writer may have good ideas, but if he/she fails to present them within a clear pattern of organization, readers will not care about how good they are. Organization helps readers to read. It creates expectations that must be met. An essay without a title, for example, is like a road without a sign. Yes, the road will take readers where the writer wants them to go, but a sign gives them some direction at the start. Also helpful are mile-markers along the way, such as paragraph transitions and thesis-support structures, to guide readers through the essay. | A writer should provide a discernible essay structure, including a title, an introduction, a body, and a conclusion that are developed in a logical, sequential order with clear transitions. Evidence should be organized within each section. An essay with good development includes supportive reasoning and evidence that **build** on each other as the document unfolds. |
| **Requirements:** the specific parameters of the assignment, including length, format, documentation style, rhetorical situation, research apparatus, etc. | A writer who does not meet the *minimum* assignment requirements fails to establish *ethos*. For example, a writer who turns in a three-page paper instead of the required five-page paper is telling the instructor, whether fair or not, that he/she<br><br>• does not care enough about the assignment,<br><br>• procrastinated,<br><br>• and/or did not put much thought into answering the writing prompt.<br><br>Meeting minimum requirements is important. | A writer should meet the minimum requirements, of course, but also exceed the instructor's expectations for the assignment by<br><br>• relying on more than the required number of credible secondary sources and being creative with the research (e.g., field research),<br><br>• exploring the topic rigorously and comprehensively,<br><br>• and demonstrating mastery of source integration (quotation blending, paraphrasing). |
| **Style:** the way in which words and sentences are put together. It involves word choice, sentence structure, and tone. | A writer should avoid words that are inappropriate for his/her audience: slang terms, offensive language, colloquial expressions, clichés, and trite phrases. A writer should not sound conversational, unless the instructor has indicated otherwise. | A writer's style should be effective for the rhetorical situation. The last thing a writer should do is alienate the audience, so he/she must choose words carefully and maintain academic register. |

| | **Undermine *Ethos*** | **Establish *Ethos*** |
|---|---|---|
| **Grammar, Mechanics, Punctuation:** the control of sentence-level errors | A writer must edit his/her work. Excessive and egregious sentence-level errors—such as misspellings, typos, fragments and run-ons, pronoun and S/V disagreement, etc.—distract readers and hoard their attention so they are not focusing on the writer's content. Readers may interpret sloppy editing, moreover, as ineptitude. | A writer's message must have strong *logos* and *pathos* to be convincing. But mostly error-free prose allows readers to focus on the *logos* and *pathos*. |
| **Audience:** the group of people to whom the essay is addressed | A writer unaware of his/her audience will not know how to present the argument and what types of evidence to include. Moreover, the writer will not be able to respond to the rhetorical needs of the audience, and more than likely will alienate them. A lack of audience awareness, in fact, impacts each of the previously listed categories. | A writer aware of his/her audience will<br><br>• use audience-based reasons,<br><br>• provide fair-treatment of alternative positions,<br><br>• and strive to rely on shared values.<br><br>A writer who understands his/her audience, and from where they are coming, will utilize strong *logos* and *pathos,* which ultimately will enhance *ethos*. |
| **Secondary Sources:** | A writer who relies on sources like Wikipedia, to provide support and information, loses credibility with his/her audience. Other sources with weak ethos may include personal (as opposed to professional) blogs, free essay websites, and comment boards. Some sources may have good ethos in some situations but are weak in others. For example, a writer analyzing the novel *The Road*, by Cormac McCarthy, should choose a scholarly article about the novel, from one of our library databases, instead of a film review of *The Road* to support his/her analysis. Finally, biased sources should be avoided, or at least handled carefully. For example, a study paid for by the International Coffee Organization may point out the health benefits of drinking coffee. ICO's vested interest in the coffee industry, however, might lead some to think the study is biased, or at least not as objective as it should have been. | A writer who uses effective secondary sources in an essay considers the following when researching:<br><br>• the credibility of the sources in terms of the audience and the rhetorical situation,<br><br>• the relevance of the sources to the topic and the writer's approach,<br><br>• and the accuracy and recency of the sources.<br><br>Also, particularly with argumentative papers, a writer gains credibility when he/she uses sources that fairly represent opposing or alternative viewpoints. Finally, as with all evidence, the writer contextualizes, integrates, documents, and explains the source material. |

*Ethos* is important. Use the information in this section to guide your decisions on writing projects. A healthy appreciation for *ethos* will help you address your audience in the most effective ways possible.

## PATHOS

*Pathos* appeals to emotions, as well as the beliefs and values of an audience. Derived from the Greek word for "suffering" or "experience," an appeal to *pathos* calls upon readers to identify with the writer's point of view. *Pathos* evokes the sympathetic imagination of an audience, where readers feel what the writer feels by "suffering" with the writer.

Let's say someone is writing about the need to require school uniforms in public schools. The writer cites the cost-effectiveness of uniforms as one of her main points. Not only might the readers disagree with the writer's stance; they might come from an entirely different socio-economic background. Thus, it may be difficult for the audience to identify with the writer's dire financial situation. In order for the readers to "experience" or "suffer" with the writer, the writer might explain how, after making sure that her four children do not go to bed hungry, barely enough money is left to pay for heating their small apartment each month. She may go on to explain that the one hundred year old building's insulation does little to protect them from "the icy hell that is a Chicago winter." The writer has appealed to the sympathy of her audience, as readers imagine themselves fighting off the notorious Chicago freeze. If barely enough money is left to pay for heating, how can a single mother expect to continually buy new school clothes for her four growing children? Readers may be further persuaded when learning that local clothing stores have agreed to place the uniforms at an affordable price, while even allowing for payment plans.

Writers can appeal to any number of emotions. Consider television commercials that ask for donations in order to feed starving children. What images do you see? What music do you hear? If people are talking, what are they saying? What emotions do you experience?

Diction (word choice), too, affects the *pathos* of an argument. The figurative language used in the first example ("icy hell") prompts you to imagine how your body would feel under such cold conditions. Diction can also negatively affect the author. If you are analyzing an essay found in *Humanity* magazine, and the essay argues that homeless shelters need to be shut down, you know because of the intended audience (people who are interested in helping others) that the essay has a big hill to climb. Let's say the author uses the word "bum" instead of "homeless person." Will that strike a positive chord emotionally with the intended audience? Not likely. In fact, it will emotionally distance the writer from the audience. Consequently, diction can tell us about an author's purpose and feelings. During a campaign speech, a politician refers to a proposed bill as "that unnecessary albatross." Through his diction, we (the audience) can gather that he will not be voting for said bill.

Humor can be a highly effective means of getting the audience on the writer's side. Super Bowl commercials are full of this kind of *pathos*, which is obviously extremely effective. Often, humor can be used when touching on difficult subjects. We see this in satirical works. As with any emotional appeal, however, humor can also backfire. The writer must know the audience's values in order to understand what kind of emotion will work in the situation. If the audience is hostile to the writer's position, humor might be a good tool; however, humor at the audience's expense probably isn't a good idea.

## LOGOS

Fred, a once-rambunctious child, who delighted in irritating his parents, had matured into a reasonably well-adjusted and respectful sixteen-year-old. Over the years, his parents disciplined him consistently and appropriately when he broke their rules. For example, when he was five, he used his father's cordless sander to write his name in the hardwood floor of the living room. Of course, they were glad to see that his spelling was correct and that his cursive script was, even on that large scale, clear and pleasing to the eye. Nevertheless, they spent time explaining to him why he was wrong to vandalize the floor, and they grounded him from some of his toys, from dessert, and from other privileges for a week. After the week had passed, Fred told his parents that he would never again use the sander to write anything on the floor or elsewhere.

There were other incidents, too numerous to recount here. Suffice it to say that, after each one, his parents punished him. The years of correction and discipline molded and shaped him, until finally he seemed to be in a good place, or so his parents thought. Fred, they believed, had reached a place of critical discernment whereby he was able to determine the possible outcomes of his potential behaviors and actions. On one occasion, he strongly desired to use the lawnmower to write "Fred+Amy=Love" in the front yard. But he quickly discarded the idea because he knew that his parents would ground him, thus preventing him from taking Amy to the movies on Friday night.

Fred thought logically about this situation. He knew that his parents historically had punished him when he broke the rules. And he knew that in this case—even though his parents had not articulated a specific "don't use the lawnmower to write messages" rule—they would punish him. If they had always punished him for doing X, where X equals breaking their rules, then completing X now would result in Y, where Y is punishment. This chain of reasoning, it should be pointed out, always assumes that his parents found out about X.

Unfortunately, he stayed out two hours past his curfew on Friday night. Yes, he knew he would be punished, and he was, but sometimes logic is not enough. Sometimes emotions (or young love) get the best of us, which is why *pathos* may trump *logos* in some situations, with certain kinds of audiences and subjects. Generally, however, *logos* should be present in an argumentative paper.

*Logos* is an appeal to logic or reason. So what makes reasoning correct? It depends. Often, something might appear to be reasonable but in fact is not. For example, flipping through a magazine, you run across an advertisement for toothpaste. You see, prominently displayed across the bottom, the following: "9 out of 10 dentists recommend this toothpaste." "If dentists recommend it and they know what's good for teeth," you might think, "then I should use it." Also included in this chain of reasoning is the following:

- Dentists are in the business of improving and/or maintaining gum and teeth health.

- They would not recommend a product if it were ineffective.

It seems perfectly rational, then, to conclude that you should purchase the product. However, look at the claim more carefully. What is the toothpaste being recommended over? What if the question put to the dentists was this one: Would you recommend X toothpaste over not using toothpaste? Or what about X toothpaste over congealed milk? No doubt nine doctors would recommend X toothpaste in those scenarios. Some consumers, however, will not think this hard about an advertising claim. In this case, the *ethos* derived from dentists creates the presence of *logos*, and that is logic enough for some.

When you are writing argumentative papers, you need to be aware of how *ethos* and *pathos* can influence your *logos*. If you are able to establish your credibility convincingly, then readers are more likely to find you and your arguments reasonable. If you are able to manipulate your readers' emotions to your ends, then their favorable response to you would seem highly logical to them.

All that said, you still need to focus on how you can add *logos* to your argumentative papers. (Review the handout "Identifying Rhetorical Appeals in Written and Visual Arguments" in this text for quick reference.) In a proposal paper about addressing obesity, for example, *logos* would come in the form of the following:

- Expert testimony from medical professionals on the physiological and psychological dangers of obesity

- Credible medical studies that provide data that illuminate the dangers of obesity

- A definition of obesity by a reputable source (medical encyclopedia, Center for Disease Control)

- Comparative studies (obesity in other countries)

- Large-scale surveys of eating and physical activity practices

You could use the Amarillo College library databases to find this information. In *CQ Researcher*, you would find an extensive report on obesity, published in 2010, that provides an overview of obesity with background and data. Additionally, the report has an extensive bibliography of resources that you could use in your paper.

Improving the *logos* in your paper, however, is not just a matter of finding convincing, reasonable, and credible sources, though that is a big part of it. You also need to think about how to sound reasonable. Using discipline-specific language, for example, may help you come across as someone who knows what he/she is discussing. Fairly considering and representing other viewpoints help you to sound reasonable, too, though here *ethos* and *logos* are working together.

Finally, strong *logos* is a result of good focus and organization. You must have a clear thesis with discernible thesis-support structures in an argumentative paper. The thesis should direct the rhetorical flow of the entire paper, and the support structures, or your topic sentences, should a) go back to the thesis, and b) provide the main idea of the paragraph. Each element of the paper, moreover, must build upon the thesis, and the elements should be arranged in the most convincing and logical way. *Logos* is much more than merely citing an article from a scholarly journal. For additional help with *logos*, particularly with how to identify errors in logic, go to *http://owl.english.purdue.edu*.

## *KAIROS*: A MATTER OF TIMING

Joe's prom is coming up, and he's a little short on money. Sure, he has a job, but he doesn't get paid until after the prom, so he decides to borrow money from his parents. The only thing is when to ask. What do you think?

a.  His mother has just come home from work, groceries spilling everywhere, the house in a mess, the phone ringing, and she is clearly angry.

b.  His mother is gone shopping, and his father is watching his favorite team that has just blown a big lead and lost the game.

c.  His parents are arguing about income taxes and an unexpected bill they just received.

d.  His father has just come home, and he is beaming about the bonus he just received from work.

Here's another scenario. Mark and Shelly received their income tax refund, and Mark has definite ideas about how to spend it: a brand new High Definition TV. He has been dreaming about one ever since his favorite team made it to the Super Bowl last year, and all he has now is the old set his parents handed down to him ten years ago. The question, though, is when to bring up the subject with Shelly who isn't really interested in television and prefers saving money for family vacations. When should Mark approach Shelly?

a.  Mark finds Shelly throwing up in the bathroom.

b.  Shelly and Mark are at her favorite restaurant, and she is gushing about how happy she is with Mark.

c.  Tired and upset from a bad day at work, Shelly walks in and flops down on the couch.

d.  Shelly has just gotten off the phone with her meddling mother-in-law.

What we've been talking about here is *kairos*. It's all about timing. *Kairos* means the timing of the argument. If you play *kairos* right, you come in at the right time with the right thing to say. If you miss your timing, you have misplayed the *kairos* of the moment, and all your *logos*, *ethos*, and *pathos* may be for naught.

Keep in mind that *kairos* also involves what you say and not just when you say it. As you might imagine, then, *kairos* is the heart of comedy. For you *Seinfeld* fans, George Costanza's "jerk store" comment from "The Comeback" episode provides quite the study in *kairos*. Would it have been more effective if his comeback were given at the right time? For those of you who haven't seen the show, George is in a meeting, and he's stuffing his mouth with shrimp while not realizing the faux pas of talking with his mouth full. A fellow employee cracks, "Hey, George. The ocean called, and they're running out of shrimp." All of the employees in the meeting laugh hysterically, and George is clearly upset, but he can't think of the right comeback at the time, so he sits and stews while trying to smile. Of course, later on his way home, he realizes the perfect comeback, and so he plots to somehow recreate the event so that he can deliver the great comeback: "Well, the jerk store called, and they're running out of you!"

Finally, George gets his chance to deliver the "great" comeback with much fervor, gusto, and self-satisfaction; however, the guy unexpectedly zings him back. George is momentarily stung. In desperation, he returns ineffectually with, "Well, I had sex with your wife!" creating an awful use of *kairos* when George immediately finds out that the man's wife is in a coma. George can't win.

Clearly, this episode is all about *kairos*. The "jerk store" comeback, as bad as it is, cannot happen without recreating the moment because George's failure to deliver the comeback the first time means that the timing has been lost, and then when George tries to recreate the moment and its *kairos*, it backfires ironically due to poor *kairos*s of another sort: the timing of the wife being in a coma. Incidentally, you may be interested to know that this episode is also about *ethos* and *pathos*. Jerry buys a tennis racquet just because the salesman seems like he might be a good tennis player; this is *ethos*. Kramer decides to create a living will all because he sees a movie with a woman on life support; this is *pathos*.

So how does all of this apply to your Comp I class? You may be asked to analyze *kairos* in an advertisement. An example of good *kairos* would be a pharmaceutical company advertising its allergy medicine in the March issue of a magazine. Why? It's allergy season, of course. Another example of good *kairos* would be an electronics company advertising its new TV in December. One reason is that it's Christmas. The other reason is that it's football season, and the Super Bowl is right around the corner. Indeed, TV commercials are all about *kairos*. Watch TV with your kids, and you'll see commercials for all the toys they love. This is audience awareness, yes, but it is also *kairos*: coming in at the right time with the argument.

*Kairos* can appear in an essay, too. Essays that use current sources demonstrate a good use of *kairos*. Essays that use old sources show a writer out of sorts with what has recently been said about a subject; perhaps the writer is even ignorant of something important that has recently been said on the subject. Of course, this is also *ethos*.

Writers that take on a hot topic are also maximizing *kairos*. Let's say that for some reason there is a rash of dog attacks that have very publicly made the newspaper over the last few weeks. A writer wanting stronger leash laws would maximize the *kairos* of the moment by writing a letter to the editor of the newspaper immediately while the shock is still on the reading audience. Failing to write in now would mean that the topic would grow cold, and then no one would care; thus, the *kairos* is off, and the argument won't work.

In short, *kairos* can be just as important as any other rhetorical element. If the timing is off, the argument may not work at all, and you may come across as George Costanza, the all-time best seller at the jerk store.

## SAMPLE WORKS-CITED PAGE FOR ENGLISH 1301

Note: Most of the following sources were created to be examples only. Also, note that website URLs are now optional; therefore, please check with your instructor for his or her preference.

*Works Cited*

Ames, Julia. *Standardized Testing.* New York: Pantheon, 2001. Print.

Edwards, Robert. "The Argument for School Uniforms." Current Debates in Education. Ed. Mary Ellen Williams. New York: Prentice, 2000. 45–50. Print.

Hall, Trish. "IQ Scores Are Up, and Psychologists Wonder Why." *New York Times* 24 Feb. 1998, late ed.: F1+. *InfoTrac Newspapers.* Web. 5 Oct. 2009.

Jost, Kenneth. "Rethinking the Death Penalty." CQ Researcher 11 (2001): 945–68. *CQ Researcher.* Web. 5 Oct. 2009.

Pillard, Richard. "The Causes of Homosexuality Are Probably Genetic." *Homosexuality.* Opposing Viewpoints Ser. Greenhaven, 1999. N. pag. *Opposing Viewpoints Resource Center.* Web. 5 Oct. 2009.

"Promoting a Culture of Life." *DISCovering U.S. History.* Online ed. Gale, 2003. N. pag. *Student Resource Center.* Web. 15 Apr. 2009.

"Public Smoking Bans." *CNN.com.* Cable News Network, 3 Aug. 2009. Web. 10 Nov. 2009.

*Explanation of Works-Cited Entries*

| | | |
|---|---|---|
| 1. | Ames, Julia: | Book with a single author. |
| 2. | Edwards, Robert: | Article from a book with an editor. |
| 3. | Hall, Trish: | Newspaper article found in AC library online database *InfoTrac.* |
| 4. | Jost, Kenneth: | Article found in AC library online database *CQ Researcher.* |
| 5. | Pillard, Richard: | Article found in AC library online database *Opposing Viewpoints.* |
| 6. | "Promoting": | Article with no author provided found in AC library online database *Student Resource Center.* |
| 7. | "Public": | Article from a website with no author provided. |

**English
1302**

# RHETORICAL ANALYSIS OF FICTION

All writing is communication, and fiction is no exception. When creating a work of fiction, an author chooses a particular setting, specific characters, plots, themes, etc., to bring compelling points and ideas to a reader's attention. When we examine fiction "rhetorically," we look carefully at these particular choices, made from an almost infinite number of possible choices, and ask, "Why this choice? What difference does it make in how we perceive the story? How does it seem to contribute to the message the author is communicating to us?"

Rhetorical analysis can help students become better critical readers of fiction because it helps them to focus on 1) a work of literature as a <u>message</u> an author is <u>communicating</u> as well as 2) the <u>strategic choices</u> the author makes to communicate this message <u>effectively</u>. Learning to analyze fiction rhetorically can help students analyze other messages rhetorically as well: "Why was this car ad shot on a deserted coastal road where speed limits don't seem to apply? Why does an attractive woman appear at the end of the ad? Why does this politician keep using the term 'far right' in his speeches?" Rhetorical analysis can also help us become more effective communicators and more aware of the choices we make when we write to convey our ideas to a reader.

## RHETORICAL ANALYSIS WORKSHEET

1. What is the <u>title</u> of the work? What does this title prompt the reader to focus on or wonder about?

2. Who is the <u>author</u>? When did he/she live and in what part of the world? Does your textbook or another source provide biographical/historical information that seems important? Who was the author's <u>audience</u> when the work was written?

3. What is the setting? Note, as specifically as you can from the information provided in the story, the location, time period, and season in which the story takes place. Does the author choose to name a specific location? Think about the effect this choice could have on our perception of the story.

4. From <u>which point of view</u> is this story told (i.e., first person, third person limited, third person omniscient, third person objective)? Who is telling the story? How does this choice affect our perception of the story? (It might help to consider how we could hear the story differently if told from another character's point of view.)

5. Identify and describe the <u>main characters</u>. What does each main character focus our attention on because of his/her unique characteristics? Are these characters dynamic or static? If dynamic, is a character's epiphany involved?

What does the character realize in this epiphany? Does a character's change bring out any important ideas? If static, is a character's resistance to change portrayed as a strength or a weakness?

6.  Provide a brief plot <u>summary</u> so that you are clear on what actually happens in the story.

7.  Identify the major <u>conflicts</u> in the story—the type of conflict (i.e., person vs. person) and which characters are involved.

8.  Identify possible <u>symbols</u>. Are any objects or places emphasized, mentioned repeatedly, and linked to certain ideas? Do any of the characters seem to stand for something beyond themselves? Does the author associate them with larger concepts? Note any evidence from the story to support your conclusions.

9.  After considering all of the information you gathered above, what do you think is the work's <u>theme</u>? (What message seems to be created through all of these particular choices?) Make sure that no part of the story contradicts your conclusion.

10. Is this work <u>effective</u>? In your opinion, does the work accomplish what it sets out to do? Is a message communicated clearly? Does it use logical, emotional, and ethical appeals (logos, pathos, ethos)? Explain.

## GUIDELINES FOR READING/INTERPRETING A POEM

1.  Determine the form/structure of the poem. What type of poem is it (lyric, narrative, dramatic monologue, sonnet, etc.)? Is there a rhyme scheme, or is it blank verse or free verse?

2.  What is the literal situation of the poem? Describe the setting and what exactly is happening.

3.  What are the characteristics of the speaker and any other people in the poem?

4.  Paraphrase the poem. Look up any unfamiliar words to help in this process.

5.  Examine the figurative language (figures of speech). Does the poem use personification, similes, or metaphors? Is the entire poem an extended metaphor? Identify and explain.

6.  Examine the poem's imagery. What type of imagery predominates? Is a pattern of imagery present?

7.  What symbols does the poet use? What is the dominant symbol (or symbols) around which the poem is based? Explain what you think they are meant to represent.

8.  Listen to the sound of the poem. How does any rhyme or meter reinforce the poem's concerns? Does the poem contain alliteration? Assonance? How do these elements enhance the poem?

9.  From the literal situation and the use of metaphor, symbolism, etc., what conclusion can you draw about the poet's theme? That is, what message/ viewpoint is he/she trying to get across to the reader? Make sure your conclusion is not contradicted by any detail in the poem.

10. What is the overall effectiveness of the poem? Does it accomplish well what it sets out to do? Does it present its message clearly? What type of impact does it have on the reader?

## BASIC GUIDELINES FOR LITERARY ANALYSIS PAPER (WITHOUT RESEARCH)

Here are some basic guidelines to get you started on a paper analyzing a short story. At this point, you might want to pick a tentative topic and do some initial reading and note-taking.

### WHAT IS A LITERARY ANALYSIS PAPER?

In a sense, a literary analysis paper is an argument paper. You will formulate a thesis about a literary work or works and defend this thesis with evidence from the work. In this paper, you will gain experience in formulating a plausible opinion about a literary work and defending it on your own.

### DEVELOPING A TOPIC AND THESIS STATEMENT

Make sure that you choose a **focused** topic appropriate for this assignment. Remember that there are many possible critical approaches when analyzing literature. If you focus on the symbolism of a particular work, for example, you are using a formalist approach. If you focus on how women are presented in a work, you are using gender criticism. Your **approach** defines your framework and helps you decide what to look for when taking notes on your work. Without a limited framework, you wouldn't know what to take notes on and would be overwhelmed with possibilities. Once you have chosen an approach and have developed a topic, you need to formulate a **thesis statement**—an assertion about the work that must be defended with evidence.

For example, let's say you decide to use a formalist approach and choose the topic "The Theme of Conversion in 'A Good Man Is Hard to Find.'" This would be a formalist approach because you would limit your framework to the story itself, not concerning yourself with the author's life or the time period which it was written, etc. After looking over the story and taking notes on the grandmother's conversion experience, you might come up with this thesis: "The theme of conversion is presented through the grandmother, who moves from a state of selfish absorption to a realization of her communion with others." Then, your burden would be to prove that the grandmother *is* selfishly absorbed, using evidence from the story, and that she *does* indeed undergo this type of transformation. You need to support this assertion because another reader might question your position, arguing that the grandmother does not really undergo any significant change.

## OUTLINE

It is a good idea at this point to create at least a tentative **outline** so that you can determine the scope and organization of your paper. Following our example, your outline might look like this:

I.   Introduction

Thesis: The theme of conversion is presented through the grandmother, who moves from a state of selfish absorption to a realization of her communion with others.

II.  Selfish Absorption

   A.  Manipulation

      1.  Evidence from story

      2.  Explanation of evidence

   B.  Self-image

      1.  Evidence from story

      2.  Explanation of evidence

   C.  Interference

      1.  Evidence from story

      2.  Explanation of evidence

   D.  Deceptiveness

      1.  Evidence from story

      2.  Explanation of evidence

III. Conversion

    A. Vulnerability

        1. Evidence from story

        2. Explanation of evidence

    B. Moment of Grace

        1. Evidence from story

        2. Explanation of evidence

IV. Post-Conversion

    A. Attempt at communion

        1. Evidence from story

        2. Explanation of evidence

    B. Misfit's reaction

        1. Evidence from story

        2. Explanation of evidence

V. Conclusion

## HOW TO GATHER EVIDENCE

Once you have a thesis statement and an outline, you know exactly what type of evidence you need to gather. For our example, you would begin gathering evidence for each section of your outline. Some students like to use notecards, while others like to type notes on the computer. Either way, be sure to use your outline Roman numerals on top of your notes so that you know which section of the paper the notes are for. Make sure that you also record the page number on which the story evidence appears. You will need to indicate to your reader which page (or line for poetry and act/scene for plays) can be consulted for the passage discussed.

## WRITING FORMAL ESSAYS IN THIRD PERSON

Below is an introduction to a piece written by Dr. Mike Bellah for the newspaper, where first person voice is acceptable, and a revised introduction for a formal English essay, where one needs to use third person. Note the differences between the two (they do not all concern third person) and then answer the questions that follow.

*Hard Choices*

"Two roads diverged in a yellow wood," writes Robert Frost, "and I—I took the one less traveled by, and that has made all the difference." Frost's poem has been a favorite of mine, but maybe not for the reason you think.

Most people seem to interpret this poem as a tribute to the road less traveled, as an endorsement for the decision to plow new ground, to explore new territory, to try or to create something new. And, I admit, this is both an inspirational theme and a viable interpretation of the poem. Yet it seems to me that Frost emphasizes the road *not* taken, as opposed to the one *less* taken. In fact, the poem is titled "The Road Not Taken." This is a poem about a common struggle we all face in life: the inability to do two mutually exclusive things. Frost says he wants to travel both roads, but he "cannot and be one traveler." So after a wistful look down the road he won't take, he sets out on the other. Of course he keeps the first for another day. "Yet," he says, "knowing how way leads on to way, I doubted that I'd ever be back."

What a poignant line! Haven't you felt this? I have. My list of roads not taken is long.

\* \* \* \* \* \* \* \* \* \* \* \* \* \* \* \* \* \* \* \*

"Two roads diverged in a wood," writes Robert Frost, "and I—/ I took the one less traveled by, / and that has made all the difference" (18–20). Well-known authors, such as Dr. Scott Peck, have interpreted this poem as a tribute to the road less traveled, as an endorsement of the decision to plow new ground, to explore new territory, to try or to create something new. Yet while this take on Frost's words may be an inspirational theme, it is not a viable interpretation of the poem. A careful reading will show that Frost emphasizes the road *not* taken, as opposed to the one *less* taken. In fact, the poem is titled "The Road Not Taken." This is a poem about a struggle common to all human beings: the inability to do two mutually exclusive things. Frost has the poem's speaker say that he wants to travel both roads, but he "cannot and be one traveler" (3). So after a wistful look down the road he will not take, he sets out on the other. Of course he keeps the first for another day. "Yet," he says, "knowing how way leads on to way, / I doubted if I should ever come back" (14–15).

1. Note the changes between the first and second drafts.

2. Explain why these changes were made.

3. The last paragraph in the first draft is not revised. How might you revise it?

**Hint: If you have trouble writing in third person, you might write the first draft in first person and then revise it.**

---

## SAMPLE POETRY EXPLICATION

*Chasing the End of Suffering: A Brief Explication of "The Childless Father"*

'Up, Timothy, up with your staff and away!

Not a soul in the village this morning will stay;

The hare has just started from Hamilton's grounds,

And Skiddaw is glad with the cry of the hounds.'

—Of coats and of jackets grey, scarlet, and green,

On the slopes of the pastures all colours were seen;

With their comely blue aprons, and caps white as snow,

The girls on the hills made a holiday show.

Fresh sprigs of green box-wood, not six months before,

Filled the funeral basin at Timothy's door;

A coffin through Timothy's threshold had past;

One Child did it bear, and that Child was his last.

Now fast up the dell came the noise and the fray,

The horse and the horn, and the hark! hark away!

Old Timothy took up his staff, and he shut

With a leisurely motion the door of his hut.

Perhaps to himself at that moment he said;

'The key I must take, for my Ellen is dead.'

But of this in my ears not a word did he speak;

And he went to the chase with a tear on his cheek.

—William Wordsworth

One suffering yet persevering father alone in his community comes from the William Wordsworth poem "The Childless Father," written in 1800 for the second edition of *Lyrical Ballads*. The father in this poem is reminiscent of Simon Lee, another Wordsworth father well acquainted with the hunt. **He differs from Simon Lee, however, in that while he is still physically able to hunt, he no longer has a joy for it. The reason for this lack of joy is what drives the poem: the death of his last child.**[a]

**Wordsworth initially describes the happy little scene in Blakean fashion, with an air of innocence and sing-song rhythm.**[b] He begins the poem with the narrator calling Timothy, the Childless Father, to the hunt: "Up, Timothy, up with your staff and away!" (1). All are going to the hunt, the rabbit is on the run, and the dogs bay in ecstasy. Excitement is in the air. Next, he catalogs the beautiful colors of jackets, coats, slopes, pastures and girls in their "blue aprons and caps as white as snow"—all part of the "holiday show" (7, 8). In the third stanza, however, Wordsworth inserts the image of a tiny box-wood coffin. The reader learns that just six months before today, the coffin containing the last of Timothy's children lay inside his house. Life abounds in the revelry of the hunt that symbolizes the life of the village in sustenance and survival; however, juxtaposed is death symbolized by a child's coffin. Amidst life, there is always suffering for the Wordsworthian father.

**But the hunt will not wait for his suffering to end.**[c] Bounding from the image of the tiny child coffin, Wordsworth moves back to the present action of the hunt in the fourth quatrain. Written in couplets of iambic tetrameter, it reads like a Christmas poem with joy all around: "Now fast up the dell came the noise and the fray, / The horse and the horn, and the hark! hark away!"(13–14). But the sadness is wholly *internal* and certainly *eternal* for Timothy. As in "Simon Lee,"

---

a. Thesis

b. Topic Sentence

c. Topic Sentence

the suffering is not abated by the community as it should be in Wordsworthian poetics. Even the narrator cannot penetrate it this time, for he can only speculate the cause of the tear as Timothy leaves this same house that once held his child's coffin: "Perhaps to himself at that moment he said, / 'The key I must take, for my Ellen is dead'"(15–16). And the reader is left to speculate further. Is Ellen the child, or do we have knowledge of Timothy's further despair? It would seem that since he must lock the door, no one is left. Perhaps Ellen is the deceased wife.

Either way, life goes on for Timothy. The hunt must continue though he has no one to hunt for but himself, and he must join it and bear his grief in silence, not disturbing the scene of Christmas joy, the eager dogs and the girls in white caps. The father must suffer alone, and he must continue on. His wife and children are gone, but he is still a father: the paradoxical Childless Father whose strong arms could not hold his family together like Wordsworth, who could not hold the memory of his daughter Catharine in his sonnet "Surprised by Joy." He must suffer, yet he must persevere, and he must do both alone. This is the suffering Wordsworthian father, and this is his task: to remember the child and bear the grief.

Wordsworth, William. "The Childless Father." *Lyrical Ballads*. Eds. R. L. Brett and A. R. Jones. 2nd ed. New York: Routledge, 1991. Print.

## QUOTING AND PARAPHRASING FROM A SHORT STORY

In your first literary analysis paper, you will use examples from the short story for evidence to support your points. Evidence might consist of only one word that you think is significant, or it might consist of several sentences. It is effective to both <u>quote this evidence directly</u> and, at times, to <u>paraphrase</u> it. Remember to <u>discuss the significance</u> of any quote or paraphrase. Don't assume that your reader will know what you "see" by using it. When you discuss a story, stay in <u>literary present tense</u>, since the events in a story are "always happening" as we read about them.

QUOTING

When you quote directly from the story, you must always <u>introduce</u> the quoted material. This means that you never let a quote stand alone but lead up to it as in the following examples. Always use <u>quotation marks</u> at the beginning and the end of the quoted material. After the quotation marks, you should put <u>parentheses containing the page number</u> on which you found the material. If the quotation ends the sentence, put a <u>period after the parentheses,</u> not before them. Try to <u>smoothly incorporate</u> quotations into your own sentences.

SAMPLE

Dee's mother reveals that Dee "was determined to stare down any disaster in her efforts" (312). She also remembers that Dee "wanted nice things" (312), though her mother had very little money. The mother sums up her daughter's character when she says, "Hesitation was no part of her nature" (311). Clearly, Dee is depicted as a strong-willed person who puts herself first.

**NOTE:** When you use *says* or *writes* to introduce a quotation, follow it with a comma, as in the previous example.

SAMPLE

The first description of Emily supports this idea of a woman suspended in time: "She looked bloated, like a body long submerged in motionless water, and of that pallid hue" (92). The water is described as "motionless" because Emily is still stuck in the past and has not accepted the passage of time. By noting that her body looks "bloated," Faulkner conveys that this attitude leads to an unhealthy deterioration.

**NOTE:** If you use a complete sentence to introduce a quotation, it should be followed by a colon, as in the previous example.

**Do NOT use quotations that require more than four typed lines in a short essay.** Don't try to reach your two-page minimum by using large "chunks" of quotations. Most of the sentences in your paper should be <u>your own points</u>, supported with short quotations. You should also know that quotations of over four typed lines require a different format.

## PARAPHRASING

Paraphrasing means that you mention an example from the story but don't quote it directly, word for word. You must still use a page number after the paraphrase:

SAMPLE

The reader is told that the smell develops two years after Emily's father dies and soon after Homer Barron left her (93). By killing Homer Barron, Emily is determined to be the one in control of her destiny, something she did not manage with her overbearing father.

The mother daydreams about appearing on a television show where her successful daughter Dee will embrace her and tell her how grateful she is for her help (311). This daydream reinforces the idea that Dee has not, in fact, accepted her mother or expressed gratitude for her sacrifices.

## SAMPLE LITERARY ANALYSIS ABSTRACT

**Thesis:** In Joyce Carol Oates's story "Where Are You Going, Where Have You Been?" Arnold Friend represents both a savior and a satanic figure for Connie.

In this paper, I plan to demonstrate that Oates characterizes Arnold as both a savior and a satanic figure to represent the attractive and dangerous sides of the "land" Connie is beginning to discover. I hope to show that, through Arnold, Oates indicts the superficial values of Connie's culture. First, I will use evidence from the story to show how Arnold seems to be Connie's savior, the type of young man that her society has built up as ideal. Oates associates Arnold with religious imagery and connects Arnold to Connie's pseudo-religious quest, which Oates describes before Arnold appears on the scene. Then, I will show how Oates invests Arnold with satanic-like qualities, which become prominent when Connie starts "seeing through" his attractive disguise. In my conclusion, I will link Arnold to Oates's purpose, which I believe has to do with an indictment of twentieth-century America's superficial values and spiritual emptiness.

## SAMPLE ANNOTATED BIBLIOGRAPHY

Below is a sample annotated bibliography. Note that the beginning of the first paragraph is the full entry of the source in MLA format. A summary of the source immediately follows. Quotes and parenthetical citations are encouraged here since they may be used in the research paper the student is working on. (In other words, the annotated bibliography functions as the student's notes on the source.) The second paragraph is the student's evaluation of the source and explanation as to how the source could be used. Students are encouraged to use third person throughout the document. Hanging indentions are also required just like they are on a works-cited page in MLA format.

Watkins, Daniel P. *Sexual Power in British Romantic Poetry.* Gainesville: U of Florida P, 1996. Print. This study attempts to demonize the poet William Wordsworth by comparing him to the Marquis de Sade. In particular, it looks at the figuring of Dorothy (Wordsworth's sister) in his poem "Tintern Abbey" as Wordsworth's attempt to enslave her in what Watkins calls "an immutable cultural and ideological landscape … leav[ing] the poet … at the center of all definitional authority" (38). In other words, William Wordsworth is the omniscient author while his sister is at the mercy of his aesthetic choices. Watkins also describes Wordsworth's sense of patriarchy towards Dorothy's childishness as "an exceptionally individualized, benevolent masculinity, which, in reality achieves its energy and definition from its highly socialized relation to a subordinated and silent feminine object" (34). Of course, the "silent feminine object" again is his sister Dorothy.

This source would provide an excellent example of a critic reaching in the dark to come up with something sensational in order to get published. The idea that Wordsworth was anything like the Marquis de Sade is ridiculous. As well, Watkins makes a crucial mistake by failing to discuss Wordsworth's famous notion of the child as father of the man. Yes, the gender is male; however, one need only look at the young girl in Wordsworth's poem "We Are Seven" to see that the gender of the child does not matter. Thus, if Dorothy is childlike and innocent in the poem, in terms of Wordsworth's philosophy, she is all the better for it.

## SAMPLE WORKS-CITED PAGE FOR ENGLISH 1302

Note: Most of the following sources were created to be examples only. Also, note that website URLs are now optional; therefore, please check with your instructor for his or her preference.

*Works Cited*

Faulkner, William. "A Rose for Emily." *Literature: Reading, Reacting, Writing.* Ed. Laurie G. Kirszner and Stephen R. Mandell. Compact 7th ed. Boston: Wadsworth, 2010. 209–15. Print.

Freund, Karl. *William Faulkner's Short Stories.* New York: Pantheon, 1988. Print.

Frist, John. "Faulkner Revisited." *Interpretations of William Faulkner.* Ed. Lawrence Edwards. New York: Prentice, 1994. 50–57. Print.

"Introduction to 'A Rose for Emily.'" *DISCovering Authors.* Online ed. Gale, 2003. *Student Resource Center.* Web. 5 Oct. 2009.

Jones, Sarah. "Symbolism in 'A Rose for Emily.'" *College Literature* 15.2 (1999): 33–45. *Student Resource Center.* Web. 5 Oct. 2009.

Porter, Jane. "Faulkner's Rose." *Literature Review* 12 (2002): 15–16. *Academic Search Complete.* Web. 2 Oct. 2009.

"Remembering Faulkner." *William Faulkner Information Page.* U of Mississippi, n. d. Web. 5 Sept. 2009.

Smith, Robert. "A Rose for Emily." *Masterplots II. Short Story Ser.* Vol. 3. Ed. Frank N. Magill. Pasadena: Salem, 1986. 1530–37. Print.

Williams, Frederick. "A Confined World: Emily's South." *Southern Literature* 24 (1984): 145-50. Rpt. in *Twentieth-Century Literary Criticism.* Ed. Dennis Poupard. Vol. 25. Detroit: Gale, 1988. 399–402. Print.

*Explanation of Works-Cited Entries*

1. Faulkner, William:     A work from our literature textbook.

2. Freund, Karl:     A book by a single author.

3. Frist, John:     An article from a book with an editor.

4. "Introduction":     An article from the AC library's database *Student Resource Center.* No author provided.

5. Jones, Sarah: An article from the AC library's database *Student Resource Center*. The article originally appeared in print.

6. Porter, Jane: An article from the AC library's database *Academic Search Complete*. The article originally appeared in print.

7. "Remembering Faulkner": An article from a website hosted by the University of Mississippi. No author provided.

8. Smith, Robert: An article from a reference work with an editor. The article was written for the reference work.

9. Williams, Frederick: An article reprinted in a reference work with an editor. The article originally appeared elsewhere.

# Glossary

**Abstract**

An abstract is a condensed version of a longer piece of writing that highlights the major points covered, concisely describes the content and scope of the writing, and reviews the writing's content in abbreviated form.

**Analysis**

An analysis is a critical evaluation, usually made by breaking a subject down into parts, then describing the parts in relation to the whole.

**Annotated Bibliography**

An annotated bibliography is an organized list of sources, each of which is followed by a brief note or "annotation." The annotations can describe the content and focus of the source; suggest the source's usefulness to the research; evaluate the source's method, conclusion, or reliability; or record the writer's reactions to the source.

**APA Format**

The American Psychological Association (APA) publishes a book *Publication Manual of the American Psychological Association* that describes how to write and format papers according to APA guidelines. Disciplines that use APA style are psychology, sociology, business, economics, nursing, social work, and criminology.

**Appeals**

Speakers and writers use various strategies or appeals to persuade their audience. Three persuasive appeals are ethos, logos, and pathos.

**Argumentation**

Argumentation is a pattern of development that works to convince the reader to think or act a particular way. The structure of an argument consists of a claim (the thesis statement) and is supported by reasons which are supported by evidence or chains of other reasons.

**Attributive Tag**

Attributive tags are phrases placed before, after, or between quoted, paraphrased, or summarized material that give credit to the author and establish the author's credibility. These tags are important in showing the relationship between the author's ideas and those of a source. They act as transitional links that connect the author's thoughts to someone else's. When naming an author for the first time, use his/her full name in the attributive tag. Afterward, just refer to the person using the last name. An example of an attributive tag is:

> According to Dr. Wes Campbell, head surgeon at Texas Hospital, "[m]any patients need blood transfusions during surgery."

**Audience**

The readers of a piece of writing are the audience.

**Body Paragraphs**

Body paragraphs are the central paragraphs of an essay, and they are meant to support or explain the thesis.

**Cause and Effect Analysis**

Cause and effect analysis is a pattern of development that gives the reasons an event occurs, the results of that event, or both.

**Chronological Order**

Chronological or time order is the arrangement of an essay's supporting details in a time sequence.

**Classification**

Classification is a pattern of development that groups items according to some principle.

**Comparison-Contrast**

Comparison-contrast is a pattern of development that shows similarities, differences, or both.

**Composition**

A composition is an essay. Composition, theme, and essay are all terms that are used to mean a short piece of writing.

**Conceptual Order**

With conceptual order, the writer introduces points related to the topic and then develops and links them. An example is a writer weaving points he or she wishes to make that relate to his or her personal experience.

**Conclusion**

The conclusion is the final paragraph of an essay and provides a strong finish for the essay.

**Critique**

A critique is an essay that gives a critical review of a work of art, a play, a movie, or a piece of literature.

**Deduction**

Deduction is the process of a general observation to individual data to reach a particular conclusion. Syllogisms and enthymemes are deductive patterns of reasoning in rhetorical arguments.

**Definition**

Definition is a pattern of development that explains the meaning of something.

### Description

Description is a pattern of development where details that appeal to the senses paint a word picture.

### Editing

Editing is the process of finding and correcting errors in grammar, spelling, punctuation, and capitalization in a draft of an essay.

### Email Attachment

An email attachment is a file which is sent along with an email message.

### Emphatic Order

With emphatic order, a writer arranges the information in the order of importance. The order is usually from least important to most important, but it can be reversed. Emphatic order is often used in persuasive writing.

### Enthymeme

An enthymeme is a syllogism that has one or more unstated premises or an unstated conclusion. An example is: Socrates is mortal because he is human. This is derived from the following syllogism:

| | |
|---|---|
| All humans are mortal. | Major Premise |
| Socrates is human. | Minor Premise |
| Therefore, Socrates is mortal. | Conclusion |

### Essay

An essay is a brief piece of nonfiction writing that examines a single topic. The essay has a title, an introduction, a body, a conclusion, and a thesis statement.

### *Ethos*

*Ethos* is a rhetorical appeal that is based on the character of the writer or speaker. The speaker, or writer, creates through the words he/she chooses, as well as other features of the text, a "character" that can speak to the reader.

### Evaluation

An evaluation is based on careful observation and study and the use of specific criteria. An example of evaluative writing is reviewing a restaurant based on the criteria of the quality of the food and/or service.

### Evidence

Evidence is facts, statistics, examples, testimony, and sensory details that support the topic sentence of a paragraph or the thesis of an essay.

### Exemplification

Exemplification is a pattern of development that involves using examples.

### Example

An example is something—a story, a reference, a statistic, a fact, or testimony—that is used to illustrate an idea.

### Fiction

Fiction is a creative work of imagination. Literary fiction appears as verse, drama, or prose.

### Final Draft

The final draft of an essay is a version of a paper that is as error-free as possible and is ready to be submitted to a teacher or for publication.

### Indirect Quotation

An indirect quotation is a reference to someone's words but not a reproduction of the exact words themselves: *The doctor said that I should take two aspirin every four hours.*

### Induction

Induction is drawing on observations and particular facts and instances to reach a general conclusion. Example is an inductive pattern of reasoning for a rhetorical argument.

### Internet or Web Browser

An Internet browser is a software application that enables a user to display and interact with HTML documents hosted by Web servers or held in a file system. Web browsers communicate with Web servers. Examples of browsers are Internet Explorer, Netscape, Firefox, Opera, and Safari.

### Introduction

The introduction is the opening paragraph of an essay and is meant to stimulate the reader's interest and present the thesis.

### Invention

With invention, a writer uses strategies, such as free writing, clustering, and listing, to generate ideas for writing.

### *Kairos*

*Kairos* refers to the timing involved with the issue. Writers effectively use *kairos* when they enter the conversation with the right thing to say at precisely the right time.

### Logical Order

Logical order is an organizational method using induction or deduction to order writing. Two options are available to the writer who uses logical reasoning: (1) beginning with a general statement and then presenting specific details to elaborate on the statement or (2) beginning with specific details and follow with a general statement of their significance.

*Logos*

*Logos* is a rhetorical appeal that is based on logic or reason. *Logos* is not just statistics. Examples can include the syllogism, enthymeme, and inductive or deductive reasoning.

**MLA**

The Modern Language Association publishes two books (the *MLA Style Manual* and the *Handbook for Writing Research Papers*) that describe how to write, format, and document sources for papers according to MLA guidelines. Disciplines in the humanities use MLA style.

**Narration**

Narration is a pattern of development that involves telling a story.

**Nonfiction**

Nonfiction writing is a literary work that is an account composed of facts, true or untrue. Essays, journals, documentaries, scientific papers, autobiographies, biographies, textbooks, technical documents, and journalistic documents are examples of non-fiction works.

**Non-Sexist Language or Gender-Neutral Language**

Non-sexist language is language that attempts to refer to neither males nor females when discussing an abstract person whose sex is not otherwise determined. An example is using police instead of policemen.

**Occasion**

The occasion is what prompts a writer to write. Examples could include a teacher assigning an essay, writing a resume to apply for a job, or writing Dear Abby for advice.

**Online or Network Databases**

An online database is one that can be accessed by computers. Libraries have online or networked databases of a variety of source material. The AC library has several online databases such as *Opposing Viewpoints*, *Academic Search Complete*, and *Article First*.

**Order by Categories**

Ordering by categories is an arrangement where supporting details in an essay are grouped together by related reasons, examples, or descriptions.

**Paragraph**

A paragraph is a group of related sentences that discuss one subject. The paragraph usually begins with a topic sentence—the main idea of the paragraph—and is followed by support sentences that can tell a story, describe a scene, explain an idea, or present examples or evidence.

### Paraphrase

A paraphrase is a restatement of another author's ideas in the writer's own words and style. Even when material is paraphrased from another source, it must be introduced by a tag and cited.

### Parenthetical Citation

A parenthetical citation credits a source by noting in parentheses where the source came from.

### *Pathos*

*Pathos* is a rhetorical appeal that is based on emotion.

### Pattern of Development

A pattern of development is a method of organizing and/or supporting ideas: description, narration, exemplification, process analysis, comparison-contrast, cause and effect analysis, definition, classification, and argumentation.

### Peer Review

A peer review is a process used for checking the writing of another (peer) student to ensure the writing meets specific criteria. Peers can identify each other's errors, and then the writers can correct the errors in the revision and editing process.

### Person

Person refers to the form of pronouns and verbs that indicates whether one person is speaking (first person), is spoken to (second person), or is spoken about (third person).

### Plagiarism

According to the Amarillo College Student Code of Conduct, plagiarism is the "appropriating, buying, receiving as a gift, or obtaining by any means another's work and the unacknowledged submission or incorporation of it in one's own written work."

### Premise

A premise is a proposition in a deductive argument. It is a statement that is supposed to be true and from which a conclusion can be drawn.

### Problem-Solution Order

Problem-solution order is the arrangement of supporting details in an essay that first describes a problem and then presents one or more solutions to that problem.

### Process Analysis

Process analysis is a pattern of development that explains how something is made or done.

**Progressive Order**

Progressive order is the arrangement of supporting details in an essay according to their order of importance, usually least to most significant.

**Proofreading**

Proofreading is reading a text for the purpose of detecting errors.

**Purpose**

Purpose is a writer's reason for writing: to inform, to relate experience, to express feelings, to entertain, or to persuade.

**Quotation**

A quotation is the reproduction of a person's exact words, which are placed within quotation marks. When material is quoted from another source, it must be introduced by a tag and cited.

**Reasons**

A reason is also called a premise. A reason is a claim used to support the thesis of an argumentation essay. Reasons often are linked to the thesis with transition words such as because, therefore, since, consequently, so, and thus.

**Research**

Research is scholarly or scientific investigation. It is a search for knowledge or facts. To research is to study a subject thoroughly and present a detailed and accurate account of the subject or facts about the subject.

**Revision**

Revision is the process of reworking and improving the content, organization, and expression of ideas in initial drafts.

**Rhetoric**

Rhetoric is the art of effective communication.

**Rhetorical Analysis**

Rhetorical analysis is using the principles of rhetoric to analyze how and why a given text works the way it does and how and why it creates meaning.

**Rhetorical Situation**

The rhetorical situation is the situation in which the author writes. It contains three parts: audience, purpose, and occasion. The rhetorical situation is the flow of information from the writer to the audience with a message that serves the writer's purpose.

### Rough Draft

This draft is an initial version of a piece of writing. It is the goal of the writer of this draft to state the thesis clearly and to develop the content of the paper with plenty of details. Correct grammar, spelling, or punctuation is not as important in this stage of writing because the writer will add material, delete information, revise and edit rough drafts, usually several times, to create the finished product—the final draft.

### Search Engine

A search engine is a program designed to help find information stored on a computer system such as the World Wide Web or a personal computer. Generally, the program searches for keywords and returns a list of sites or documents that contain the keywords. Popular search engines include Google, Yahoo, and Excite.

### Source

A *primary source* or original document is one that provides unedited, first-hand facts. Primary sources can be first-hand documents, letters, contemporary newspaper accounts, or photographs. They can also be oral histories, memoirs, autobiographies, diaries, court records, interviews, research results generated by experiments, surveys, and ethnographies.

A *secondary source* analyzes or interprets primary source material. Secondary sources are prepared based on the information contained in primary sources and often explain or comment on the primary source material.

### Spatial Order

Spatial order is the arrangement of supporting details in an essay according to their order in a space, in a particular pattern, such as near to far, top to bottom, or front to back.

### Style

Style is the way a writer expresses ideas in sentences.

### Syllogism

A syllogism is a form of deductive reasoning. The syllogism contains a major premise, a minor premise, and a conclusion. An example is

| | |
|---|---|
| All pit bulls are vicious. | Major Premise |
| Marty has a pit bull. | Minor Premise |
| Therefore, Marty's pit bull is vicious. | Conclusion |

### Subject

Subject is the topic of an essay.

**Summary**

A summary is a restatement of a long passage in the writer's own words and style. Even when material is summarized from another source, it must be introduced by a tag and cited.

**Supporting Details**

Supporting details are the ideas that back up or support the topic sentence of a body paragraph or the thesis of an essay.

**Tag**

A tag is the same as an attributive tag.

**Text**

A text is the object being studied, critiqued, or analyzed. It can be a literary work, a movie, a piece of art, an advertisement, or any cultural artifact.

**Theme**

A theme is an essay. Composition, theme, and essay are all terms that are used to mean a short piece of writing.

**Thesis**

The thesis is the main idea or the central point of an essay. The thesis often appears in the introduction.

**Topical Order**

Topical order is a method of organization where an author presents several related topics and then develops them.

**Topic**

The topic is the subject of an essay.

**Topic Sentence**

The topic sentence is the main idea or point of a paragraph.

**Works-Cited Page**

The works-cited page is an alphabetical list of sources that a writer cites (makes reference to) in a paper. The list provides the information a reader uses to locate and read any sources cited in the essay.